From

Death

To

Life

Discovering Life Through Failure & Pain

Rufus Bradley Sr.

WestBow
P R E S S
A DIVISION OF THOMAS NELSON

All Scripture quotations unless otherwise indicated are taken
from the New International Version (NIV)

Other versions used are:

GNB- Good News Bible
TLB-The Living Bible
KJV- The King James Vision
CEV- Contemporary English Version

WestBow Press books may be ordered through booksellers or by contacting:

WestBow Press
A Division of Thomas Nelson
1663 Liberty Drive
Bloomington, IN 47403
www.westbowpress.com
1-(866) 928-1240

ISBN: 978-1-4497-8809-4 (sc)
ISBN: 978-1-4497-8808-7 (hc)
ISBN: 978-1-4497-8810-0 (e)

Library of Congress Control Number: 2013904515

Printed in the United States of America

WestBow Press rev. date: 03/14/2013

Table of Contents

Foreword

With all the books being written today for pastors to read on building a church or ministry, what a breath of fresh air it is to read Pastor Rufus Bradley's book *From Death to Life*, where his transparency and getting real with his readers, shine. Driven by humility and brokenness, as well as being led by the Holy Spirit, Pastor Rufus's book reveals the good, the bad, and the ugly that happens in the process of birthing a church. This is a book where the author gets real,—first with himself and then with his readers—by telling it like it really is and how he learns from his mistakes, becoming thus more fulfilled.

He first shares the initial birthing of the ministry and how this immediate time of success was purely the Lord's vision and not his own. As the ministry grew, it went through a painful period of decline, and he humbly takes full responsibility for its downfall. Pastor Rufus painstakingly sought the Lord for His divine vision and surrounded himself with wise counsel (Prov. 11:14) for the ministry, which opened up the avenue for his turnaround period, during which he continually thanked and praised the Lord for the success of the vision because of the grace that was bestowed upon him.

Pastor Rufus proceeds to take his readers on a step-by-step journey of how the Lord showed him to build" New Life Ministries," based upon the four vision pillars explained in this book. He breaks down each pillar with very practical and helpful information. What a huge help this book can be for pastors who are in the process of building a church/ministry.

In the end, he shares his vision for reaching and improving the neighborhood to become the best church for the community, humbly going before his congregation, businesses, government agencies, and other ministries so they could catch the vision. He ends on how together this can become a reality as well as a model to follow in becoming community minded and winning the world to Jesus.

Weldon Townsend

Senior Pastor of Shield of Faith Ministries

Saginaw, Michigan

Preface

As I wrote this book, I couldn't help but think about how people would respond to reading my life story. I even wondered if it was a good idea to express myself and disclose stories dealing with real-life people. The more I thought about it, the more it made sense that I should write this book because the information could truly help so many people who are struggling and don't know what to do. With this in mind, I became so excited about sharing my life story that I no longer wondered if I should write it; I was totally convinced to put the story into action.

From Death to Life is a true story that takes you on a journey and allows you to see things you perhaps have never seen, feel things you have never felt, and go places you have never been. Each page is designed to help you see the beauty or feel the pain as birth is given through the content of its pages. Each chapter is designed to make you appreciate the life only God can give.

This book is designed to help one understand how a seed must die in the earth before it can give birth to fruit, which supplies provision to so many. In a sense, death takes place, a new life begins, growth is nurtured, preparation is made, and a new idea is created, bringing people together to accomplish a common goal to make life better for others. In each chapter, the voice of God thunders loudly as He paints a picture of what can be for people who have lost hope, resulting in changed lives forever. Some of the stories are like scenes in a motion picture, bringing to reality what seems impossible to men. The stories are told for the purpose of motivation and inspiration, while the Scriptures are given for life application. This book intends to build character and increase the faith of those who want to move forward with Christ.

Acknowledgments

I have so many people to thank for their support as I searched my past to gather twenty-seven years of information and make sense of all the experiences I put into this book. First I would like to thank God for giving me the personal and pastoral experiences I have had over the years and allowing me to use them to motivate and help others. I thank my wife, Relinda, for her love, support, and patience over the years, especially during the times I had to spend away from our family to make the vision a reality. I thank my church family who stood by me as I endured the hardships of authoring a book; my writing team, who labored to help me proofread this book; and my chief editor, Barbara Watkins, who made me work to find more and to write and rewrite the work as the Spirit of God delivered it to me from chapter 1 to the end.

Finally, I want to thank all of my community development partners, who helped to give the book a good ending. By sharing their resources to make things happen, they have given life to the vision. It is because of people like these that I am confident the Lord will do even more as we continue toward a new era of kingdom ministry.

—Pastor Rufus Bradley Sr.

Introduction

The focus of this book is a prospering church that figuratively died because it made drastic changes too soon and had a lack of vision for its future. This book also reveals how God can resurrect a church from death through proper vision connection. It shows what causes death in church growth, what to avoid in the early stages of growth, what to put in place to ensure continual growth, and how God, our heavenly Father, can turn bad situations into good through the proper vision connection.

The Holy Spirit has allowed me to learn invaluable lessons for raising the kind of church that is pleasing to Him. Through my personal pastoral experience pastors across America can benefit from these lessons as they lead the flock of God through change. These lessons will serve as tools to build a well-balanced twenty-first-century ministry. These lessons will help pastors see the danger of not having a clear, compelling vision and how a vision will keep the church vibrant and growing. The lessons I have learned will also warn pastors not to take church growth for granted.

In my conversations with various pastors, mainly at the local level, there are many who admit they don't have a clear vision for their churches—only an idea. I had the privilege of sitting with a few pastors to help them put their hearts for ministry on paper. I shared with them vivid details of my own ministry so they would feel comfortable letting me help them.

I believe God is pleased with us as pastors when we share our shortcomings in ministry, as well as our successes. Most of the time in my studies I read glowing success stories on how to become successful in ministry, but I don't often read about the failures. The fact is, our struggles are just as important as our accomplishments, just as our redemption is greater than our fall; both success and failure can be used to motivate others to succeed. This information will also show people, mainly leaders, that even if they don't do well at first, or even if they fail, they can still do big things by listening and learning from God. I believe there are no wasted experiences with Him. Sometimes we waste them because we don't want to reveal our imperfections, but Christ Jesus can always use our experiences to help others. There is proof of this in Scripture.

> He helps us in all our troubles, so that we are able to help others
> who have all kinds of troubles, using the same help that we
> ourselves have received from God. (2 Cor. 1:4 GNB)

Based on this verse, I believe God intends for pastors to share their experiences with one another—the good, the bad, and the ugly. I have experienced all three, and I am ready to share with those who are indecisive about making changes and to encourage those who are at a standstill because of their fear of change. I am sharing my failures and successes, with humility, so I might help someone who truly wants to grow Christ a great ministry. I believe there are many leaders who pastor smaller churches like mine, averaging fifty to four hundred members, who are in need of such information. My hope is that they will find inspiration from my story that will help them find life-changing motivation to overcome the fear factors lying at the root of stagnancy in church growth. I also hope Christ will help them move against their fears so they can move the church into the community as God intended. This book can serve as a model for vision-implementation to help churches restore broken communities across the nation as they search for new opportunities to make a revolutionary difference in the communities in which they live. The Scripture says,

> His [God's] intent was that now, through the church, the manifold wisdom of God should be made known to the rulers and authorities in the heavenly realms. (Eph. 3:10 NIV)

To get the most out of this book, it is absolutely necessary to read it in its entirety. One must experience the good, the bad, the ugly, and the excellence of the turnaround only God can provide. Chapter 1 will describe the ministry in its prospering years; you will see fast growth and the hand of God moving in a big way. You will also see the first miracle God performed on me as a pastor, figuratively bringing me from death to life because of the work He had for me to do. Chapter 2 will reveal the declining and painful period when the church hit rock bottom because we made changes too quickly and had a lack of vision. Chapter 3 begins the turnaround period when the true vision for the church was birthed, written, and cast.

Chapters 4, 5, 6, and 7 will explain the vision pillars, their functions, and programs grown from the vision. Chapter 8 will introduce a powerful program called Shepherding, which is designed to help implement the four vision pillars into the lives of the membership. Chapter 9 will show God's preparation to move the church from building parking lots to building community. Chapter 10 will introduce a powerful community development program called Mission in the City that was created through the vision. This chapter will also speak about a community sports-and-fitness park built by the Mission in the City Movement and how it is being used to change the community in a huge way. This movement has helped eliminate the negative perceptions of the churches throughout the city by causing men to glorify God, just as Jesus said,

Let your light so shine before men, *that they may see your good works*, and glorify your Father which is in heaven. (Matt. 5:16 KJV)

Finally, chapter 11 will enlighten the reader on building partnerships with people who are waiting to help them accomplish their community goals. It will share how God will open doors to help them if they can make their vision plain and compelling as they make their requests known.

Chapter 1

The Prosperous Embryonic Period

To really appreciate this book, you must learn the entire history of New Life Baptist Church. The earlier period will set the stage for what the Spirit is going to reveal in the latter part of the book. In this first chapter, you will learn about the prosperous period of the church when everything we touched turned to gold. I will also describe several events illustrating God's favor in getting the church off to a great start.

The Phone Call

When I was an associate minister at Christ Fellowship Baptist Church, I also served as a teacher and assistant pastor. One of the deacons of my previous church called to ask me if I would be interested in pastoring a church. Apparently a few members from the church had decided to terminate their membership, and they were looking for a leader who could continue with their spiritual development. I told the deacon I truly believed God's call on my life was to be a pastor, but I could not consider their request until I had prayed about their proposal and discussed it with my own pastor.

A week later, I called the deacon back to set up a meeting with the people who were interested in my leadership. Fourteen people showed up at one of the members' homes. I stressed the seriousness of the subject and made sure they knew how happy I was with my family, my involvement with my home church, and the joy I got from preaching all over the city and out of town as people needed my ministry. I didn't want to change any of my church or home life unless the group was really sincere in their offer.

Everyone at the meeting made a covenant with God and made a commitment to me that they would be faithful members of this mission. I tested the commitment of the mission-seeking group by asking them to pay their first tithes and offerings as proof of their seriousness. We collected $407 to start the new mission. This happened around the third week in January of 1985, and on the first Sunday in February, we held our first service under the name New Life Baptist Mission. All the members honored their commitments, and the church picked up momentum very quickly. One month later, we called in a Baptist church counsel team to organize the church and were declared a certified Baptist church under the name New Life Missionary Baptist Church, with a membership of eighty-five people.

An Unfit Building

The church was located at 325 Lapeer Street in the Old Rescue Mission Building. The building was unfit for safe public worship. We had to keep buckets handy in case it rained. By hanging buckets underneath the dropped ceiling to catch rainwater, we could prevent damage to the floor and ceiling tiles. Those buckets were hung in faith, hoping none of them would fall during the worship service. The faithful men of New Life had to be at the church every Sunday morning by 8:00 after a rain to empty and re-hang the buckets before Sunday school began. Without a doubt, God was with us through all of this. No one got hurt, and the congregation never knew the buckets were over their heads. Along with a leaky roof, there was no heat in my office. Therefore, I did all of my office work at home. The building was old and in bad shape, but God allowed us to use it until we were ready to build.

Preparation to Build

As we contemplated our next step, God was already working in our favor, making preparations for the church to purchase seven lots of land to construct a new building (when the time was right). God touched the owner's heart to sell the land to the church for $2,500—all the money we had. A few members were a little concerned about the location of the property, as it was in what we called "the hood"—an area known for drug trafficking, prostitution, and gang activity. I convinced them that the hood was where God would want His church built. After much discussion, we voted to buy the land, trusting God with all the unseen details.

Due to rapid growth, the church had to make some quick decisions on how to raise the finances we needed to build a larger place to worship. Thanks to the Spirit of God and the efforts of fewer than one hundred people, we raised $75,000 for a down payment on a new building in only six months. Everyone worked very hard on our fundraising campaign. We sold steaks, fish, candy, and pretty much anything else we could to raise the money. We had birthday drives, where people who were born in certain months worked together to raise more money, competing against people born in other months. We had a lot of fun working together on these projects!

The building we had drawn up cost roughly $200,000; with our down payment, we still needed $125,000. The church's membership had grown to about 150 members, and our rapid growth was evidence that we needed to begin building. Since we had only been established for six months, we had a problem getting a bank to loan us the remaining $125,000. But God had placed a pastor on the board of Second National Bank; he spoke up for our young church, and our loan was approved.

In September of 1985, we experienced the favor of God in a major way. Thanks to Him and the efforts of 150 people, a new worship center was emerging from the earth. We worked with very little money, yet things were moving rapidly, and people were gathering weekly to watch the salvation of God. In March of 1987, two months before the building was completed, we realized we needed pews, yet we had very little money for interior furnishings. However, we prayed, and God saw the members' faith and permitted a church furniture company to meet our furniture needs by putting us on a payment plan to cover $20,000. God blessed the church to pay off this debt in six months.

The March

Shortly after the building was completed, the growing congregation marched from our former location at 325 Lapeer Street to our new church at 1401 Janes Street. This was God's third big move on our behalf in less than two years. The first was starting the ministry; the second was God's hand in taking me off my job; and now the third was that we had built a church and were marching to the new location. This march was the most amazing event of my life and the life of our congregation. We felt we had accomplished a major milestone at such an early stage, and I saw the mighty workings of God all through this movement.

I will never forget the Sunday morning we gathered to march to our new location. People from all over the community joined us on this five-block march. Law enforcement led us as a local tourist bus followed behind, carrying the elderly people who couldn't walk very far. I can still hear the words of the songs we sang: "We're Marching On," "Glory, Glory Hallelujah," and many others. We entered the new building for our first 11:00 a.m. worship service, and the Spirit was moving in a big way. Over five hundred people were packed into our new sanctuary. The theme Scripture for the morning and evening dedicatory service was taken from Zechariah.

Then he answered and spake unto me, saying, This is the word of the Lord unto Zerubbabel, saying, Not by might, nor by power, but by my spirit, saith the Lord of hosts. (Zech. 4:6 KJV)

God got the city's attention that day; He showed everyone what He could do if people would only trust Him. By the end of 1987, the church had grown to about three hundred members, with Christ adding to its growth weekly. The growth of our young church reminds me today of the early church and how God blessed it based on the loyalty and commitment of the people, as described in book of Acts.

They devoted themselves to the apostles' teaching and to the fellowship, to the breaking of bread and to prayer. Everyone was filled with awe, and many wonders and miraculous signs were done by the apostles. All the believers were together and had everything in common. Selling their possessions and goods, they gave to anyone as he had need. Every day they continued to meet together in the temple courts. They broke bread in their homes and ate together with glad and sincere hearts, praising God and enjoying the favor of all the people. And the Lord added to their number daily those who were being saved. (Acts 2:42–47 NIV)

Two weeks after the building was completed, some people expressed concerns about walking on a rocky parking lot. When it rained, the stones and mud caused a major problem for women wearing high heels. People were proud of their work for Christ, and the church and didn't want to sit in a worship service with muddy, scratched shoes. Again we prayed, and the Lord intervened and permitted an asphalt company to provide the church with $13,000 worth of asphalt. The church was again blessed to have this bill paid in six months.

The Retaliation

Shortly after we moved into our new worship center, we experienced what a few members had been afraid would happen if we built in the hood. Some people who previously had dominated the territory didn't like us building a church on their turf. After the worship center was finished, we had several encounters. They intentionally parked their cars in my parking space on Saturday nights. I found out where they lived and asked them to please move their car so I could get into my office. I put a cable across every driveway entrance in hopes of deterring them from taking my parking space. However, the next morning, we were surprised to find the cables and cement poles pulled out of the ground. One morning we discovered a window had been broken in the fellowship hall. I confronted one person and told him, "It doesn't matter what you do. You can burn the building down if you want to, but you will not take over our church." We had to stand our ground or they would have taken over the land the Lord had given us. Therefore, we stood firm.

Not too long after that, things got better, and we became friends. The mother of the family joined our church and often brought one of the family members with her, who later married a member of our church. Thank God for a great ending!

Preparation to Leave My Old Job

In 1988, the work of the ministry had grown so much that I retired from my truck-driving job to become a full-time pastor, leading the people of God in spiritual development. By this time, the church had expanded to nearly five hundred people on the roll, with about three hundred committed members, and was still growing.

Departing from my job could have been a hard thing for me to do, if Chirst had not intervened and made the transition easier for me. During this time, my job was one of the highest-paying jobs in the city, with full benefits. This meant a great deal to a man with a wife, two small children, and all the other responsibilities that come with being a husband and father. To give up all of this in hopes that the church would support me was a big undertaking. God worked this out for me way before I thought about leaving. He permitted some things to happen that would later prepare me to move when the time was right. When we started the church in February of 1985, things were beginning to change for me at my job. I was a good driver and had a great relationship with the people I provided service to, but for some reason, I couldn't please my bosses any longer.

Their actions toward me seemed as if the company had suddenly turned on me. Even the other drivers couldn't understand why they were giving me such a hard time. My supervisor had started riding along with me every day to evaluate my performance, often taking me into the office to chew me out, and I didn't understand why. Normally I served a hundred-plus customers a day, and on Wednesdays, I needed to be home early so I could teach Bible study, so I had to skip my lunch. I did whatever I needed to do to get off early.

The next day when I returned, I would find that my boss had added more customers to my route, claiming I didn't have enough work. The job became more and more impossible to do, and pleasing my boss was just out of the question. There was even a time when they made me work until midnight. I was knocking on doors in the middle of the night, and people were upset about me coming to their homes so late and disturbing their sleep. To me, this was one of the worst forms of punishment.

The Stress and Pain I Experienced

I was so depressed that I became a reckless driver. One day one of my customers gave me a message to call my boss. I made the call and he chewed me out so bad, that when I left the store, I accidentally ran into another car. I was so upset; I didn't see him coming even though I was looking. The car landed in a ditch so deep that I couldn't see it, and all I could do was cry and hope the driver came out walking. Thank God he did! I called the Equal Employment Opportunity Commission and asked them to please save me from the company's harassment, but they couldn't help because it was my word against theirs.

My life had become so frustrating and stressful; I was diagnosed with major depression and was off work while I saw a psychologist. At this time, I began to lose weight. Normally I weighed 163 pounds, but I had dropped to 143 pounds. I was also having some serious problems with my digestive system, which was interfering with proper bowel movement. My family doctor did all kinds of tests and then later referred me to a gastroenterologist, who tested my large and small intestines. The specialist could see my bowels were filled with waste but couldn't figure out why this was occurring.

They finally determined that stress had caused the muscles in my intestines, which would normally produce a vibration to keep the bowels moving, to go into "sleep mode," which meant many times my bowels wouldn't move for seven days at a time. When I got to my office on Sunday mornings, my bowels would release. One thing for sure happened on a weekly basis: I could feel the stress lightening up on Friday evening when I was leaving work and returning on Monday morning as I returned back to work. One day I called in sick, and my boss actually came to my house! He knocked on the door, and when I answered, I asked him why was he at my house. He said he came to see how I was doing. I thought this was as low as one could go in times like these to send someone to a depressed person's house to harass him more.

God's Deliverance

I never will forget the day I came off sick leave. I had to go see my doctor, and on my way there, for some reason I went the long way around and took a route that led me by my job site. As I was riding, I was moved to stop in to see my boss, and I shared with him where I was going. He acted as if he were glad and hoped I could return to work, but before I left him, he gave me a written note to give the doctor saying if he released me back to work, the company would not be responsible for any damage I might cause as a driver due to my illness and previous accident.

This let me know they knew what they were doing to me; they wanted me to quit and walk away peacefully. At this point, my doctor wrote him a note saying I could return but not as a driver. Therefore, they had to give me a part-time job unloading trucks. I stayed on this part-time job for the remainder of my employment with the company.

As I contemplated leaving my job, I spoke with a few friends who were older and had been in the ministry longer than I had. I wanted to discuss with them my decision to leave. They encouraged me to hold on to my part-time job, just in case things didn't work out with the church. This way I would still be in the loop of things with my job. I didn't accept their advice because I felt in my heart God didn't want me in the loop any longer, and if I had stayed, it would have no doubt ended my life.

I really felt like my life was over, and I knew if Christ didn't help me, I wouldn't last very long. At this point, when I was totally helpless, the Holy Spirit performed a resurrection in me, bringing me back from the dead because He had work for me to complete. Through this move, I saw the Spirit move me from death to life.

Shortly after these events, I called a meeting with the deacons and trustees to discuss becoming a full-time pastor. I let them know I could no longer be in two places at once, and I had to leave one of them. I was so glad to leave the job that God didn't have to worry about me ever bringing up the company's name or its benefits. I took a half cut in pay and was happy to wait on God to give back to me what I had given up to do His work. My wife was shocked when she heard what I was about to do, but I told her I had been challenged to trust Christ in this matter according to His Word. The scriptural basis for my decision was from these verses:

And Jesus answered and said, Verily I say unto you, There is
no man that hath left house, or brethren, or sisters, or father,
or mother, or wife, or children, or lands, for my sake, and the
gospel's, But he shall receive an hundredfold now in this time,

houses, and brethren, and sisters, and mothers, and children, and lands, with persecutions; and in the world to come eternal life. (Mark 10:29–30 NIV)

A New Beginning

From 1988 to 1990, God restored my sanity and was birthing great ideas in me for moving the church forward. Most of my time was used for teaching and creating a Bible study that would challenge people to grow in spiritual maturity. All of our classes were being taught in the sanctuary and in every other part of the church; even certain hallways were used as classrooms.

In 1991, God blessed me to lead the membership to build an impressive twelve-room educational wing onto the church to support the expanding Christian education program. This educational wing provided room to grow, both in numbers and in Spirit. At that time, Sunday school averaged two hundred students weekly and the mid-week Bible institute averaged 150 students weekly. This program focused on a curriculum consisting of several different class studies, which were all based on the needs of the people. We taught classes for singles and married couples, budgeting classes, woodworking classes, computer classes, cooking classes, and basic Bible study. People were excited about the church and the classes being taught. Even members from other churches were attending our studies.

We also had a few ministries that took us outside the church walls. We developed a sick ministry of about fifty people who met at the church weekly for training and hospital visitation. The group would then go to the hospital, and as the Spirit prompted them, they would ask people if they could pray with them. This was a very exciting ministry, and people were talking about the work in a very positive way all throughout the city.

Another ministry that set us apart was called the bereavement ministry. The workers of this ministry were trained to visit people who had lost loved ones; they would take food to their homes, send encouraging cards, and make phone calls. This group also met at funeral homes and passed out comforting information to those who were bereaved. There was also a singles ministry that helped single people find their purpose and build healthy relationships. We also had a children's ministry that worked with the children during Sunday school, worship service, and midweek service and did creative children's projects. These ministries served as our marks of distinction that set us apart from other churches and gave people reasons to attend and join our church.

In 1992 we were led to purchase a thirty-four-passenger tour bus and a fourteen-passenger van to transport people to our worship service, Sunday school, and mid-week Bible institute. The purchase of this bus also allowed us to attend state and national Congress of Christian Education conferences in many different states for higher learning, ministry-development opportunities, and implementation of church-leadership strategies. The favor of God was really upon our church.

During this time, Jehovah God blessed me to make the rewarding decision to pursue further education by committing to a five-year study program presented by the United Bible Institute in Flint, Michigan, an extension of United Theology Seminary of Monroe, Louisiana. I earned a bachelor's degree in religious education in May of 1997.

While I pursued higher education, the congregation fell off sharply due to my neglect of the flock. I had too much going on in my life. Taking on a full load at school of fifteen to eighteen hours, reading and writing papers for five years, keeping up with my family, and leading the church members was an arduous task. With these things going on, I found myself losing focus. Honestly, I just couldn't be there for all the people. I had to teach what I was learning in school, and I didn't have room for any extra in my life. There was no creativity for the church, so the people dropped off in their attendance and began to scatter to other churches. However, by 1998, the church family was back on track and growing. Shortly after bringing the ministry back together, I began to sense God's calling for me to lead New Life Baptist Church to become a life-changing ministry at a different level of operation.

A Desire for More

As you can see, we did amazingly well as a young church, purely on faith and inspiration. I had an undeclared vision locked up inside of me, but it was not enough to accomplish God's purpose for the church. Like many pastors, I had a general idea of what I wanted to do, but I wasn't sure of how to make it happen. I was confident God wanted me to lead the church to become a ministry for the whole person, but I had no idea of how to accomplish this goal. I was without direction and had no one to help me in vision development.

Not having a vision is not something a pastor really wants to divulge to others. How do you tell people you don't have a vision for your church? A good friend of mine who was a pastor counseled me one day, "I have watched you lead your church. Everything you do, God blesses." He told me he had seen me lead the church to the foot of the mountain several times but we couldn't cross. He said, "When you discovered you couldn't cross, you went back and started something new. You successfully brought the church to the foot of the mountain, and each time you couldn't cross."

I agreed with him and asked him how could I fix the problem. He said, "God will show you. Pray, and ask God to put a person in your life who can show you how to cross." I prayed as instructed, not knowing the answer to the prayer would come through several different leaders and in different ways. I will share answers to the prayer throughout the rest of this book.

As I waited on Jesus to answer, in the summer of 1999, I led the church to do a community survey seeking the felt needs of the community so we could better serve people. In this survey, we discovered there were several needs, and we got so excited. We couldn't wait to start working to fulfill those needs. The needs were: recreation, housing, child care, after-school programs, jobs, and a safe place for senior citizens.

The most amazing things happened shortly after this discovery. God took this revelation of needs and put them away for a later time, when we would be ready to use them. We could not fulfill those needs until we had gone through a very painful period of learning and training that only God could provide. Chapter 10 will detail those needs and how the Spirit used them to make a difference.

The church's story is amazing because it reflects the hand of God moving in the lives of people in a way that is completely impossible for any human to do. I share this information so every reader can sense the grace God bestows upon every person He gives a task.

Chapter 2

The Declining and Painful Period

After many years of prosperity, God permitted me to experience what I call the most painful time of the ministry, when everything fell through the cracks because we tried something the church wasn't ready for. We hit a rough spot, took a nosedive, and landed in a place that was unknown to us. The pain was severe. It came from many different directions and was inflicted by many different people. However, I learned more through this period of my pastoral experience than at any other time.

The fastest-growing church in town became the most talked about church. Suddenly it seemed like the whole city had turned against us, and our church was being criticized throughout the city. I hate to say this, but people from other churches were recruiting our members. They would ask them, "Are you still at New Life Church?" or "Are you still with Bradley?" Even those who left would ask the remaining members, "When are you coming with us?" It seemed as if the departed really wanted everyone to leave us, but God permitted a few faithful members to remain to fulfill His plan for the church. Those who stayed were embarrassed and didn't really know how to defend the church *or* me. I was hurt and didn't really understand what was happening. Our congregation had become so infected with negativity that no one would visit, and the departed rejoiced in seeing us fall.

Many talents, minds, and hearts walked out of the front door of the church, never to return. This was the worst pain I had ever experienced in the ministry. To go from the top to the bottom is not commendable. This is when you are embarrassed as a leader; when everybody is watching to see what you are going to do and whether you will quit or continue; and when people lose their respect for you. This is when you are repositioned in the community and are no longer remembered for the good you have done. This is also when people drive by your church and say, "That's the church that used to be on the cutting edge."

During this time, no one would join our church. Very few would visit, and those who visited never returned. We were cut off from almost every church in the city. No one would invite us to a fellowship or any other church function. All I could do during this time was read, write, think, dream, attend seminars/conferences, and buy land without a clear purpose, hoping God would one day let me use it for the kingdom. This period lasted for about five years. As I look back, I believe this nightmare period in ministry started because of two human errors.

First Reason for the Pain: Making Changes Too Soon

The changes I made in our ministry started shortly after I attended my first mega-church conference in the fall of 1999. I studied purpose-driven preaching and small-group dynamics under the leadership of Dr. Rick Warren and the Saddleback Church leadership team in California, gleaning information to help move our church forward. This was one of the most exciting times of my life! I was learning valuable information from a proven and successful ministry. Quickly, I saw what was possible in any church, large or small. After I returned from the conference and reviewed what I had learned, I began to use their model and to implement changes within our own church structure to help with future growth.

I changed the Sunday school to small group sessions held in members' homes. This move was designed to spread the church out all over the city. We launched ten small groups in ten different locations in hopes of winning souls from each location through Bible studies and fellowship activities. At the right time, the leaders of the groups would bring the people to the church, and together, we would baptize those who were being saved. I studied the program and felt I knew how to make the concept work for us. The program worked well for a few weeks, but it wasn't long before I discovered how much of a mistake I had made.

I didn't realize how much training had to take place before launching a program of this magnitude and how much unity there had to be among the people who were leading the groups. Leadership is the key to these kinds of programs. Everyone must be on one accord and of one mind; this wasn't the case with our ministry. In our ministry, people who didn't know one another came together. Some of them had never talked in church, yet they became best friends, and their focus became building personal friendships apart from the church. They omitted everything I had taught them about building community.

Most of these groups worked against what I was teaching, and they soon fell apart. I had to call all of them back in from the different communities. Some of them had lost respect for me as their leader due to bad company. For some reason, the program didn't work for us during that time of the ministry, but I can still feel the power of its growth and continue to use the model to some extent today in leading people to spiritual maturity. Currently our Life Development Program is built around small groups held on our church campus in houses belonging to the church rather than in the homes of individuals, and they work great. I will talk more about our Life Development Program in chapter 8.

I also changed the worship style of the church. We moved from a traditional service to a more contemporary celebratory style of worship. We put in a big screen so people could stand and sing along rather than sitting back and being entertained. We progressed from performance worship to involvement worship. Our goal was to celebrate the presence of God by standing, lifting our hands, clapping, and making a joyful noise unto the Lord. We used songs that challenged people to respond or be engaged in the worship with words like, "I will lift my hands to You, I will sing of Your glory, the glory of the King." These are involvement songs challenging people to lift their hands as they worship.

At the time, this change was not well-received because traditional churches mostly sit and worship. The traditional Baptist church is accustomed to seven-finger chords in their music with several verses in the songs, which produces more performance worship. Many people despised the new songs, and the church suffered negative publicity.

We used a praise team to get through this period because we felt it would be much easier to transition the congregation in the change. This was also not well-received because the traditional-minded members felt the choir was the number-one singing unit in the church, and the idea of having a praise team created all kinds of problems. People got upset and would not sing the songs in worship. They would stand up but wouldn't open their mouths. They felt I was changing the feel of worship by singing songs from Caucasian artists rather than their accustomed African American music. They also assumed I was trying to replace the choir with a five-person praise team. People who weren't even members of our church approached me about this move. I tried to explain that we still had the choir and we were just trying to enhance our worship service with other options, but it just didn't make sense to them. This led them to not visit our church for worship, which added to the negative reports some of the people had already put out about the church.

I must admit, I changed some things too soon, and if I could repeat it, I would do things differently. The lesson I learned is not to get too excited about what other people are doing in their church and to wait on God to show me when to move and what to change. I wanted to believe the church would follow me in the changes I made. I thought my track record for leading the church was outstanding, but after I changed several things and moved too rapidly, I quickly learned that was not the case, and I was in trouble.

In hopes of saving the declining congregation, I started another worship service, but I immediately found that you don't start new services during times like these. We were so excited as we approached the new service, and when the time finally came, the house was full, the music was great, and the message was outstanding. The new service was held at 8:00 a.m., and after that, we held our 11:00 a.m. service. It was heartbreaking to discover everyone had decided to attend the first service, leaving the second service very, very empty.

In the process of building this second service, it was disturbing to learn some of the leaders were attending only to see the service fail. They would peek through the windows, watch the cars pull up, and say things to each other like, "I knew no one was coming" or "I knew it would be like this." Never did I hear them talk about praying for the service to be a success. This was another good idea that turned out bad because of improper preparation on my part. As a leader, if you don't prepare people for change, you can expect doubt to saturate their minds, causing them to see only what can't be rather than what can be.

Making changes too soon can be devastating and very painful. If people can't see and understand what you are doing and why you are doing it, they will not follow you. Lack of understanding will produce a powerful resistance in them, which will cause severe pain. Change is one thing; transitioning is another. Change is moving something from one place to another, while transitioning is preparing people's hearts for the move.

In retrospect, I must admit I made some changes too soon and without preparing the people's hearts. As I was changing things in the church, I got several warnings from God through people, but I didn't listen. One of my preacher associates said to me one day, "Pastor, you are moving too fast. Slow down. People can't keep up with you; they are getting confused, and you are hurting the church." Of course I didn't listen; I was so caught up in what I saw could be that I didn't realize I hadn't prepared the church for all of the changes being implemented. People were leaving the church, and word had gotten out into the community.

It was all over town that New Life had taken a turn for the worse. People had left, and the church was empty. My ears were still closed to many people at this time, even the people who were trying to help me. My own pastor spoke to me one day and asked me, "Do you feel God is leading you to make all these changes?" I responded, "I really feel inspired by God to do what I am doing." What I didn't understand was that inspiration does not necessarily demand immediate action. If I had only known, I could have made the same changes without any problems over time. The Scripture says,

There is a time for everything, and a season for every activity under heaven. (Eccles. 3:1 NIV)

Change is about God's timing, not our own. In essence, there was nothing wrong with any of the changes I made during this time; I was just too early—about ten years too early. I know this because many churches throughout the city are using those same changes today. It always seemed as if I was ahead of my colleagues, and doing the work of a pioneer has always been part of my composition. I have never been afraid to go first and am always willing to test the ice before everyone else. The bottom line is knowing the right time.

Second Reason for the Pain: Not Having a Compelling Vision

The second human reason I believe this pain occurred was because I did not have a compelling vision. I have learned over the years how important it is to have vision and the danger of not having it. Without a vision, anything can happen, from changing things too soon to getting caught in traps you cannot escape.

At the time I didn't have a vision for our church that went beyond Sunday worship, mid-week Bible study, and a few ministries. Worse yet, I was making changes based on Dr. Rick Warren's vision. When you don't have your own vision from God, everyone's dream sounds like yours. You must be extremely careful how you use information and inspiration coming from another person while you are seeking your place with God or trying to find your own direction. Your vision has to be from God only, or it won't last. In George Barna's book *The Power of Vision* he says, "A vision that is not God centered may enjoy temporary success but probably will not provide a long-lasting impact."[1]

A God-centered, compelling vision will protect you for the future. It will elevate your level of thinking as you move forward. A compelling vision will protect you from moving too quickly and will show you what can be and what shouldn't be.

I remember so well a message the moderator of our district sent

---

1   George Barna, *The Power of Vision*. (Ventura, CA: Regal, 2009), 61.

me. He said, "Pastor Bradley will make a great leader one day, after he has suffered and gone through the pain of becoming a leader." The moderator was totally convinced I had grown too fast and missed out on leadership development. Today when I think about it, I know the message was correct and sent from God. As a pastor, I didn't have to suffer anything to grow the church to five hundred members. God blessed everything we did. People came to the ministry with excitement. When I look back now, I see what the moderator was talking about, for truly the pain was ahead of me. I did not see what was coming. I really do believe this man was a prophet sent from God with extraordinary wisdom, and when he spoke, things happened. He spoke those words regarding my future, but I didn't listen.

Sometimes young pastors move faster than their thinking ability. Wisdom comes from experience, and you don't get all of the wisdom you need at one time. This is why young pastors need to be mentored by older pastors. Seasoned pastors have the wisdom to provide the young with leadership advice that will help them pastor their churches more effectively.

I truly did not have a compelling vision. I wasn't even thinking about vision. I came from a church where vision was not talked about in this manner. I pastored the church based on what I believed, what I saw, and what I had been taught. Because of my beliefs and what I was taught, I faced trials of many kinds. I know now that if you don't have a vision that is clear and convincing, you will be destroyed. Most pastors have some kind of vision but not necessarily a clear and compelling idea that will change people's lives. Leaders are quick to say we have a vision because we would be embarrassed to say otherwise. As I stated several times, my vision was limited to Sunday school, mid-week Bible study, Sunday-morning worship, and a few ministry areas, and within these few areas, we did very well. Traditionally speaking, all pastors have these ministry areas in common; in fact, they are the main focus of every traditional Baptist church. They all speak highly of the big three: Sunday school, Bible study, and worship service. These are like programs to help make the vision become reality once it has been discovered.

I was not really sure if my limited vision was enough to take us to the next level of growth or even protect us as we grew. As a matter of fact, I once had a student in Sunday school who cried out he was going home to do harm to someone who had wronged him. The Sunday school teacher was so concerned about teaching the lesson he didn't hear the statement. As a result, the man went home and did just what he said and was in trouble for a very long time.

A compelling vision for the church would have required the teacher to meet the man's troubling needs. Because of this incident alone, I knew something was wrong with how I was developing the lives of people. If I had cast a clear vision to the teachers and they had caught it, there is no doubt the teacher would have ministered to the distraught man in the class on a one-on-one basis because the most important thing would have been to help him. If we were truly going to meet the needs of the people, then this is one need the teacher should have never ignored.

Any part of a vision will produce some progress, but a compelling vision that's bigger than you and well-articulated will change people's lives. Not to have a vision at all is a different story. To not have a vision is to not have a future. I've heard it said over and over, "A nowhere destination always results from a nowhere plan."

A compelling vision is a description of what can be. It's a picture you paint as you explain what God is speaking to you. The picture is so convincing that when people draw it up in their minds, the picture creates within them a burning passion and produces an energy, driving them to make something happen. Vision connects people with the impossible and provides them with the hope to fuse their future.

If you cannot see in your spirit where you are going and how it will look when you get there, it simply means you are not going anywhere, and your ministry will be unproductive. Without a vision, there is nothing to dream about. Your dreams are birthed from your vision, which is the future you see regarding the church. We dream to make the vision become reality, and in the process, the church will grow broader into the community and meet the needs of the people. If you are not dreaming, something is in the way; maybe it is a lack of vision.

If a leader can't see where he is going, he will not be able to effectively get anyone to follow him. The leader and the follower will only go in circles, and the people he commissions to help him will fail every time. In these situations, a leader is likely to engage in unproductive pursuits, just to say he is moving. The lack of a compelling vision will hurt you in many different ways, which can turn out to be very painful. When I look at all the things that happened to me, it helps me to better understand what it really means to not have a vision. "Where there is no vision, the people perish" (Prov. 29:18 KJV).

To not have a vision is to say there is no order; people are uncontrolled, unrestrained, and out of hand. When a church is having these kinds of experiences, several things can be working together to distort the progress of the church. It all results from not having a clear vision. To give you a clear idea of my meaning, I want to share a few of them from my own experience:

It Will Cause the Church to Be Sinful

Without a clear vision in place, sin will run rampant because there will be nothing to keep the church moving forward in a positive way. In my situation, I was open to all kinds of gossip and listened to things that were counterproductive to the call of preaching and pastoring. My focus was more on who said what than preaching the gospel of Jesus Christ.

I was more focused on chasing down rumors, and most of my energy was split between trying to convince people to accept the ministry and trying to prevent people from destroying what was left of it. These kinds of vain actions really helped me to understand the importance of having a clear vision.

An unproductive environment will blind you to any possibilities for the ministry and the foresight of God's desire for the church. When the leader can't see God's idea for his church, the people perish. To perish is to allow crime and sin to roam uninhibited, leaving people confused, frustrated, hopeless, and without a future. If there is no hope to draw strength from, both the leader and the members will be robbed of their drive and passion to keep moving forward. The church will become sinful and allow evil to become the dominant force within its structure.

This is the time when people don't care about each other, they lose respect for the things of God, and a spirit of deceit is formed, causing them to lie and gossip uncontrollably. When sin runs wild, people don't care who they hurt. You have to watch every word you say or your words will be used against you. This kind of negativity will empty a church—quickly. God is my witness! I experienced some horrific things in the ministry just because I did not have a compelling vision to lead and protect me from making mistakes. However, things could have been a lot worse if God's grace hadn't kept me and preserved me to be used gloriously at a later time.

It Will Cause You to Lose Focus on Your Purpose

Without a vision, you don't have anything to focus on to keep you on track. I was so busy trying to save the church that I stopped using wisdom. I used all my energy trying to keep the few members I had, and I stopped thinking and lost focus on God's purpose for me as a leader.

One day a young lady came to me with a deep wound another member was inflicting on her in her home life. I knew quite a bit about the member in question, and I shared with her information about the lady I had learned through pastoral observance to convince the woman not to invite the interfering member back to her home again. I was wrong, even though my intent was to save this family from future tragedy.

It is sad to say, but the young lady I was trying to help told the other member what I said, and this caused all kinds of problems that I still regret. This scenario caused me to lose four families from the church, and I really didn't have members to spare. This is the result of not having a compelling vision to protect you. Vision would have led me to handle this differently; I would have never used the person's name or shared what I knew. Vision will keep you clear of messy situations, and it will show you how to deal with them in a more profound way, protecting you and everyone else involved. If helping someone is going to give you or the church a bad reputation, it may not be good, and if it is good, you won't have any regrets.

It Will Make You Lose Focus on Your Family

When you don't have vision to protect you, you can so easily lose focus on your family. I still regret how I spent so much time away from my wife and children, trying to make everybody else happy. Most of the people I neglected my family for don't even attend my church any longer. I see it so plainly now, but back then I was blind. We as a family could have done so much more together, and I still would have had plenty of time to pastor the church. As a matter of fact, spending quality time with family is part of the duties of a pastor. I thank God that I did some great things with my wife and children. Really, I think I am the one who was affected most by not being there as I should have been.

It Will Cause You to Start and Stop with Ministry

A lack of vision will cause you to start and stop, like a flock of geese without a leader. Geese will take off with a strong notion to go somewhere and then turn around and come back to the lake or pond. This process is repeated until they choose a leader or get direction. As a pastor, one can so easily spend one's whole career starting and stopping and never lead the church into its mission. You can be good at doing so much but never succeed. As my pastor friend said, he watched me bring the people to the foot of the mountain in everything I did as a leader, but we never crossed. I would just start all over with something else. If you don't know where you are going, you'll never know how close you are to arriving at your destination. If things don't seem to be working in one idea, you will just stop and do something else. This is the action of a visionless thinker.

It Will Cause You to Overlook the Good You Already Have

During this time, God had blessed the church by putting us in a unique position as the youngest church in the city. People all over town were excited about the youthfulness of the ministry. I was the youngest pastor in town, and God made the church a magnet. I had great members of the church—community leaders, white-collar workers, and people who could have helped me grow into a mega-church ministry—but I didn't realize what I had until it was too late humanly speaking. I didn't realize how important it was to have quality people working with me in the church.

For example, my budget administrator, who served with me for ten years, was gifted in accounting and could produce any kind of financial data we needed. She later left to become a supervisor of accounting in a different city. I also had several ministers who were very skilled in church administration, teaching, and preaching. Currently three of them are leading cutting-edge churches in different cities in Michigan. All those gifts were given to me to build the ministry, but I didn't realize what God had given me until later and they had already moved on to lead their own ministries. All of this happened because I didn't know where I was going. Together we did some great things, but they were not according to vision. The help I had was ready to go forth and produce, but they couldn't go any further than I could lead them.

It Will Cause People to Become Angry

The folly of making changes too soon and not having a clear vision caused the church to develop into three different groups, all of them upset.

One group got angry and left. One of my own relatives came against me in a meeting she wasn't even supposed to attend. After I asked her to leave, she challenged me on what would happen if she didn't. We exchanged a few words, and she decided to leave New Life and join another church. Her departure affected her husband, and he also left to be with her. Later on, others went and joined them.

I will never forget the day following a Thanksgiving service when my budget administrator and her family got up after the closing prayer and walked out the front door. This was surprising because she had never used this door to depart from worship. The moment I saw this, I knew she wouldn't be back. Upon returning home, I called her, and she opened up and revealed they were moving their membership. I really think she may have left because I replaced her with a person who was more available than she was because of her work schedule. Sometimes people don't like to give up their spots. With all the things going on, I couldn't think clearly enough to wait until the storm was over before I moved her.

Another group got angry and stayed. Their goal was to put the church back like it was so everybody could come back home and the church could be like it had always been. They did dirty things to stop the church from refocusing, which ultimately caused even more people to leave. They would go behind my back to destroy the few relationships I did have with people. They would bear false witness and report things I did not say to some of the members.

As I look at things now, I can understand their anger. Change is hard. For quite a while, I thought I was the only one who was hurting, but I was wrong. People really don't want to do something different if they love what they are already doing. Making changes is hard enough as it is, but not making them correctly will affect the membership more negatively.

In Dale Galloway's book, *Leading in Times of Change,* he said, "People feel awkward and self-conscious doing something new." He also quoted these words: "People focus on what they have to give up. People want to know how the change will affect them—how will they fit, what will they miss, what visibility will they lose, how much will it cost them, and will they still be needed."[2]

In other words, if people are convinced the change won't be in their favor, they are going to resist it no matter how beneficial it can be. You must show them how they can benefit from the change. I know this from experience.

Last, another group was angry at the sin yet trusted God and the leadership. This group was determined to stick it out and prayed for God to help us keep moving forward. They surely loved the new changes and wanted everybody else to join in and let me lead. When others stopped believing, they saw the best in me. They couldn't believe the people

---

2   Dale Galloway and Beeson Institute Colleagues, *Leading in Times of Change.* (Kansas City, MO: Beacon Hill Press, 2001), 30–31.

had turned their backs on me. You will see the outcome of this group's action and how God used them to make a difference in the community in chapter 10.

It Will Cause People to Disrespect the Leadership

A high-ranking leader in the church no longer accepted my leadership as being relevant to his family. I realized this when his wife had to have a very major surgery and he didn't bother to ask me to pray for her. As a matter of fact, neither one of them told me the surgery would be taking place. I saw him the same day of the procedure at the church, and as he walked by me, I spoke to him, but he never said anything about it. The sad part was, he had told most of the members and was even reporting to one of them as the surgery progressed. When I spoke to him about it, he couldn't justify his actions, and I had to relieve him of his duties.

I will never forget the day when my only daughter got married. Most of my leaders purposely did not attend her wedding, claiming they forgot. It was a hurtful feeling I had never experienced before. It was during these times I truly understood the power of disunity in a church. Some people had driven over 150 miles to attend this wedding while the leadership of the church forgot. For my leaders to simply disregard this event was unimaginable, and performing my own daughter's wedding with this on my mind was not an easy task. That's the kind of sin that destroys from within. At that point, I thought it couldn't get lower than that moment.

One man even had the audacity to tell me he was keeping his tithes and offering at home in a drawer, and when I put things back like they were, he would give them to the church. As sad as it was, I told him we were not going back to the beginning. I asked him to tell me what he thought I was doing wrong. He said I had taken the pulpit out of the church by turning it into a stage "to do theatrics" and that I had quit preaching and was doing too much teaching. He felt this way because I didn't use the singing type of voice when closing my sermons.

I had to release teachers who would go into the classrooms and turn the people against me. They misconstrued what they heard me say to make people dislike me. They even used my house as an example to make others disrespect me by comparing homes and prices. They accused me of drinking and doing all manner of things against the will of God.

Also, during these times, people thought they could do whatever they wanted, even to the point of blatantly disrespecting me as pastor. One person in particular decided to change the order of service without my permission! After I confronted her, her words to me were, "Maybe this isn't the ministry for me." My natural response was, "It's probably not." I suppose she felt as if the Holy Spirit could no longer use her in our ministry.

Musicians heard our church was going through a hard time and thought we would allow anything to save ourselves. Many of them applied to help the ministry, but it turned out that nine out of ten were only interested in finding money for their pockets. They had very little respect for our ministry. Every musician I employed eventually had to be discharged, which caused them to go out into the community and relay all kinds of evil against the church. They told people no one could work for me and it was my way or the highway. They gave me a new name in the community: the hatchet man.

I brought in a man from another church who was gifted in dealing with numbers. He loved to see the bottom line and to research data to ensure everything was in order and on schedule. After being a member for about year, I put him on the trustees ministry to work as an auditor of finances. His task was to ensure the budget was on schedule and that we were financially secure. He worked with a long-time member of the trustee board, and together they presented their first report to the trustees.

They also gave me a report on the suggested cuts needed the keep the church on schedule. As it turned out, most of those cuts pertained to my benefits package, which I had for twelve years. A good vision would not have allowed a relatively new person to be placed on a ministry of this magnitude. When I read the report, I knew immediately whose voice I was hearing, and it wasn't the voice of the trustees who had been working with me. Somehow the new member of the trustees board had manipulated them into doing something highly embarrassing. In the best interest of the church, I released him immediately. Shortly afterward, he took his wife and children, who had been members for twelve years, and together they joined another church.

In Dale Galloway's book *Leading with Vision*, he makes this crucial point:

> Never, never surrender your vision to negative thinkers. Every church has a member or two who always sees the gloomy side of an issue or sees an attack dog behind every bush. These dear brothers and sisters have to be loved, and served as a person for whom Christ died. You must realize that a glass ceiling can be put on an entire congregation by a few negative thinkers. Be pastoral to them, but do not allow them to pollute your spirit or contaminate your faith. Since negative thinkers usually do not or cannot change much, it is usually not advisable to spend much time trying to fix them.[3]

---

3   Dale Galloway and Beeson Institute Colleagues, Leading with Vision.(Kansas City, MO: Beacon Hill Press, 1999), 75.

It Will Cause the Church to Have a Negative Reputation

In the midst of all this chaos, the church picked up a negative reputation in the community. We became a church where people no longer trusted the ministry, and this trend lasted for about four or five years. They felt the church was no longer a safe place to invest their lives for spiritual development. Many went out and made the claim that I had lost my mind and declared the members who remained with me were crazy. I really felt bad for the church and for myself. As I look back, I see this negative reputation was being built for at least twelve years before the crash.

In the beginning, during the prosperity years, there was an iron-fist type of leadership some people despised. I didn't build good relationships with the members. We were the youngest church in the city, but I did not make good use of a life-changing opportunity to become a cutting-edge, large church. I couldn't correct people without making them my enemies. I would cut people down from the pulpit.

When people missed church for three months, we would call them and try to get them back. If they did not return, I would send them a letter stating, "We haven't seen you in three months. Our records show that either you have left us or you are not responding to our attempts to connect with you. Therefore, we are giving you thirty days to let us know your position." If members were missing because of work-related issues, I would send a letter stating their tithes would show if they still had an interest in the church until they were able to return. I felt this was the right thing to do. I let them know if we didn't hear from them, we would assume they were no longer interested in membership, and their names would be removed from our records. Thinking back, this wasn't a good idea because it was uncompassionate and served as a weapon for people to use against me. The members didn't like it, and they discussed it indignantly with other people in the community.

I had to learn these things the hard way. From time to time I would hear things people were saying about me, but I didn't pay much attention. They said things like, "This church is too hard," "Pastor needs to learn how to talk to people," or "People are afraid to express themselves to him." They feared being embarrassed. I really think this kind of attitude comes with not knowing what to do or where you are headed; it's a defense mechanism to keep people from finding out that you don't know.

The bottom line is, when I failed in the transitioning period, I had so many people who didn't like me because of my past disposition. When they heard things were going bad for me, they said, "He is getting what he deserves." News of my controlling spirit had spread into the community so relentlessly that even when I wanted to change, it wasn't accepted. There is one thing you should know: if you are going to rule with an iron fist, remember that you can never make mistakes, because if you should mess up, the people will use the same iron on you. Your past will catch up with you no matter how tough you are.

At this point, I was ready to talk to someone. I needed to express how I was feeling. I needed someone to tell me what I had done wrong. I hoped someone could give me some wisdom on how to correct myself. Everything people had tried to tell me in the past was now revisiting my mind as I went through this lacerating and excruciating pain that progressively became worse with time.

I will never forget one day when I was visiting a member of the church at the hospital and ran into a senior pastor I knew. I opened up to him, and he said to me, "You changed too much at once." Then he encouraged me to pray for God to show me how to get back on the right track.

I asked God to let me leave and allow someone else to rebuild the church. As the founder of the church, this was a hard thing for me to ask. I felt I had let God down, along with the members of New Life, and

I didn't deserve to continue as the leader of the church. Every part of me was crushed. I felt I could do a better job for God in another place, but at the same time, I didn't want to go.

I sent out resumes to other states to see if I could find an opportunity to lead another church. Many of them loved my resume and talked about bringing me in for an interview, but for some reason they never came through. They even thought I was the kind of person who was an answer to their prayers. God had a plan for me, and I just couldn't see it clearly. I thought that I had messed up so badly I was finished, but He wouldn't provide me with an opportunity to leave New Life Baptist Church. Christ had a plan all along to remove the negative reputation I had created, and it wouldn't happen until later in my life. I had to sit still and keep working until God fixed things. Only Christ can change the effects of a negative reputation.

When I look at what is happening now in the ministry, I fully understand why God wouldn't permit the move. I had to stay in the location where the death took place so God could perform a resurrection among the people who knew about what had happened to the church and its pastor. If I had left town, there wouldn't have been a resurrection. Only the people in my city would be able to see and understand the power of the church-and-community resurrection that came through the vision He gave me for the future. When I look back, I see God using my past pains and experiences to prepare me for a twenty-first-century ministry where vision and change would be a top priority in the church. Through it all, I am so thankful for God's correction so I could become the kind of leader who can help others. The Scripture really makes it plain on what God can do with our pain.

Sometimes it takes a painful experience to make us change our ways. (Prov. 20:30 GNB)

Through my pain, God was putting things in place. I was having experiences, learning valuable lessons, connecting with the right people, and learning how to become a visionary leader who would one day lead New Life to become a cutting-edge ministry as God planned the turnaround for the church. The pain I went through was the tool Christ used to birth the vision He had for the church. This school of hard knocks was a learning experience only the Holy Spirit could teach. The miraculous experience was like a mother giving birth to a child. Through the pain, I was able to see the light. I shared this information because I don't want to see what happened to me happen to any other pastor. Every pastor needs to determine his or her vision or direction for his or her church right away. If you don't, you may not get another chance, as God gave me.

Chapter 3

The Turnaround Period

𝔍n this chapter, I will share how God turned things around for the church and me through a vision connection. The pain was over now, the lessons had been learned, and a new birth was ready to take place in the ministry. I was ready for Christ to fill me with a new direction that would set the church on a life-changing path.

In 2003, I was convicted to do as Habakkuk did: climb into my watchtower and see what the Lord would say to me.

> I will stand upon my watch, and set me upon the tower, and will watch to see what he will say unto me, and what I shall answer when I am reproved. And the Lord answered me, and said, Write the vision, and make it plain upon tables, that he may run that readeth it. (Hab. 2:1–2 KJV)

As I heard the Lord speak, I began to write as He gave me direction for turning the church around. After all the trials, I truly felt a passion to build a ministry to meet the needs of the whole person. The vision still wasn't clear, but I felt a deep conviction this was the kind of ministry God wanted me to lead, though I knew I would have to go through more learning processes before it became clear. It was at this point various leaders began to help me as an answer to my prayer, and I was ready for the challenge of learning.

More Training

In the fall of 2003, I received some information in the mail from the Beeson Institute regarding advanced church leadership training. It was led by Dr. Dale Galloway of the Asbury Theological Seminary, and it encouraged me to enroll in a three-year leadership training program. I know this information was sent from God because prior to receiving the mail, I was talking with one of my pastor friends, and he gave me a brochure about the very same program and encouraged me to attend with him. The next day I received the information from the school itself. I had no idea who gave them my name, but I knew this was a confirmation from God to attend as part of His answer to my prayer.

From there I enrolled in the program and studied under the personalities of nine mega-church leadership teams in nine different states to learn how to effectively lead a church, with some focus on community development. Several other pastors and I were challenged to enhance our leadership skills.

In 2004, I studied "How to Mobilize the Laity" at Frazer Memorial Church in Montgomery, Alabama, under John Ed and his leadership team. This study helped us see the importance of including lay people in developing life-changing ministries. Some of the areas of focus were using the laity to pray for the congregation, caring for the sick, training ministry leaders, studying and teaching the Bible, telling people about Jesus, representing the church at events, running errands for the church office, and encouraging people through hard times. All of these things will help fulfill the Great Commission of Jesus Christ. Involving people in ministry will help build a high-impact church. When ministry is shared by others, it multiplies and produces excitement throughout the entire body of the church. This idea is well supported by the following verses:

> Two are better than one, because they have a good return for their work: If one falls down, his friend can help him up. But pity the man who falls and has no one to help him up! Also, if two lie down together, they will keep warm. But how can one keep warm alone? Though one may be overpowered, two can defend themselves. A cord of three strands is not quickly broken. (Eccles. 4:9–12 NIV)

In 2004, I studied "Healthy, Winning Staff Teams" at the Church of the Resurrection in Kansas City, Kansas, under the leadership of Adam Hamilton and his leadership team. This study taught us how to recruit the right staff for growing a healthy church. This training opened my eyes to the fact that we as leaders cannot hire people just because we know them. Hiring people should be based on the vision and those who have the same philosophy of ministry. I learned if the people we hire don't share the same values as us and possess a passion for the work, then we are wasting God's resources.

I learned that the purpose of staff is to make things happen, so as leaders we should hire people who can do what we can't do so we are not forced to micromanage the work. One big thing I learned in this study was the importance of hiring the right person, because it is much easier to get people into a position than it is to get them out it. This piece of information helped me tremendously.

I had hired a person to lead our worship who couldn't produce what we needed to impact the service. This person seemed to be one of the world's greatest musicians, but we needed far more than music. We didn't know how to fix the problem without causing further problems because the members had gotten so accustomed to the music. We had to wait for many years before God showed us how to fix the problem. I learned in this study that if you don't know how to release people, you can cause bigger problems due to relational and emotional connections built with the membership. I believe this Scripture speaks clearly on how to avoid these kinds of problems.

Get the facts at any price, and hold on tightly to all the good sense you can get. (Prov. 23:23 TLB)

In 2004, I also studied "Small Groups and Need Meeting Ministries" at the Ginghamsburg Church in Dayton, Ohio (Tip City), under the direction of Mike Slaughter and his leadership team. During this study, we explored the power of small groups and learned they are nonthreatening to the people. Small groups are designed for people to grow as they build relationships with one another. In these groups, people feel safe sharing their lives as they learn the Bible. It has been proven that more care can be given in small groups, as they open multiple entries into the church. Small groups can also be placed in the homes of people in every community. They can be a great form of evangelism and a safe place to fellowship, learn, share, experience God, and minister to one another, as seen in the following verses:

Those who accepted his message were baptized, and about three
thousand were added to their number that day. They devoted
themselves to the apostles' teaching and to the fellowship, to
the breaking of bread and to prayer. Everyone was filled with
awe, and many wonders and miraculous signs were done by
the apostles. All the believers were together and had everything
in common. Selling their possessions and goods, they gave
to anyone as he had need. Every day they continued to meet
together in the temple courts. They broke bread in their homes
and ate together with glad and sincere hearts, praising God and
enjoying the favor of all the people. And the Lord added to their
number daily those who were being saved. (Acts 2:41–47 NIV)

In 2005, I was blessed to study "Worship, Preaching, and
Transitioning," at Christ Church in Ft. Lauderdale, FL, under the
direction of Phil Roughton and his leadership team. This study elevated
our level of thinking relating to communicating the Word and leading
people to worship God. The most emphasis was placed on transitioning
the church so it would be current in ministering to people in today's
world. This study pointed out the importance of moving the ministry
from maintenance to mission. Emphasis was also placed on the role of
the pastor to be on the cutting edge as he leads the church in change,
lest the church become outdated and die. In other words, the church
must be a change agent—a place where Jesus can invest new wine.

Neither do men pour new wine into old wineskins. If they do,
the skins will burst, the wine will run out and the wineskins
will be ruined. No, they pour new wine into new wineskins,
and both are preserved. (Matt. 9:17 NIV)

Again in 2005, I studied "Balancing Your Personal Life" at the Gaylord Opryland Hotel in Nashville, Tennessee. In this study, we learned about the importance of balancing time between our wives and the church. We looked at some of the pitfalls with marriage and ministry, such as making the church the top priority instead of making our marriages the top priority. They taught us the importance of having fun with our spouses and to not let anything interfere with our relationships. We were warned as pastors not to run off to do church work when situations at home need our attention. This study made me realize how far off track I had been in my marriage and how much I had already neglected my wife; yet, the training showed me how to get back on track before it was too late. This information was anointed and supported by the Word of God.

> Now as the church submits to Christ, so also wives should submit to their husbands in everything. Husbands, love your wives, just as Christ loved the church and gave himself up for her. (Eph. 5:24–25 NIV)

In 2005, I also studied "Building Blocks For An Effective Church" at South East Church in Louisville, Kentucky, under the direction of Bob Russell and his leadership team. In this study, our focus was on the steps necessary to build an effective church. A few of the steps we needed to have in place were: the lordship of Jesus, visionary leadership, healthy leaders, teaching of Scripture, compelling worship services, prayer, and many others, counting on God to direct us as the Scripture tells us.

> In his heart a man plans his course, but the Lord determines his steps. (Prov. 16:9 NIV)

In 2006, I studied "Visionary Leadership" at Christ Church of the Valley in Phoenix, Arizona, under the leadership of Don Wilson and his leadership team. In this study, our eyes were opened even more to the need for vision and visionary leadership for the church. A church can't go any further than its leader can see and won't go any further than its leader's faith. The leader must have faith to serve as evidence or proof for what he believes is going to happen. Faith is seeing what can be before it becomes a reality, according to this verse:

Now faith is the substance of things hoped for, the evidence of things not seen. (Heb. 11:1 KJV)

Once the leader sees where he is going, he is able to paint a picture or draw a map, showing people what it looks like and how to get there. The picture he paints will connect people to the idea and energize them to move forward with the vision. I was inspired in this study to create ways to communicate a vision and to cast and recast my vision to the people. I learned how to develop slogans and vision symbols and how to connect them with teachings, programs, and ministries. This study taught me how to break the vision down into manageable parts so I could set goals and develop one part at a time. It also helped me to clearly see whom I could delegate the work to at every point. Vision shaping is too big for one man alone; he will need other people to get excited about what God has shown him, as exemplified in the following Scripture:

After Paul had seen the vision, we got ready at once to leave for Macedonia, concluding that God had called us to preach the gospel to them. (Acts 16:10 NIV)

In 2006, I studied "Church for the Un-churched" at Willow Creek Ministries in Chicago, Illinois, under the direction of Bill Hybels and his leadership team. In this study, we learned about the characteristics of a healthy and growing church. This kind of church must have clear vision, and the vision must come from God to the leader. I was given great insight during this time of study. It helped me to understand what makes people follow leadership. I have been told when people buy into the vision, they buy into the leadership. If we want to reach the un-churched, we must equip the church to be able to turn around and extend their hands to reach others. As the church brings in new people for Christ, there must be a place for them in the body or they won't be around long. If we are to be a church for the un-churched, we must lead them into their rightful place of ministry, according to their giftedness. This is the kind of church that makes room for new people by sharing the work with them. This idea is plain in Scripture.

> It was he who gave some to be apostles, some to be prophets, some
> to be evangelists, and some to be pastors and teachers, to prepare
> God's people for works of service, so that the body of Christ
> may be built up until we all reach unity in the faith and in the
> knowledge of the Son of God and become mature, attaining to the
> whole measure of the fullness of Christ. (Eph. 4:11–13 NIV)

Finally, in 2006, I studied the "Purpose-Driven Church" at Saddleback Church in Irvine, California, under the leadership of Rick Warren and his leadership team. In this study, we learned about the importance of being purpose driven in our churches, with plenty of emphasis on core values as a way to protect the church and give purpose to the church. I learned that if you do not know what you value in your church, you will never know if you are on course. Everything we do must be done with purpose. You can't effectively run a church unless all your leaders have bought into the core values and use them in the ministries they lead. Core values are principles we don't break, bend, or compromise at any time for any reason. When we practice our values, God will establish our thoughts, as the Scripture teaches.

Commit thy works unto the Lord, and thy thoughts shall be established. (Prov. 16:3 KJV)

Throughout this training, I was inspired to read many books, which put me in the direction where God was preparing me to lead the church. The books I committed myself to read the most were written by Dr. Dale Galloway and the Beeson Institute Colleagues. These men are amazingly great teachers, and I highly recommend any leader who wants to build God a great church to read these books before going any further in your vision-casting. If I had read these books before I started making changes, things would have been done entirely differently. I continued this three-year program and graduated in 2006 with a sealed certificate of completion. In addition, over fifty members from the church attended several of the training sessions with me to assist me in leading the church in a new direction.

Midway into my studies with the Beeson Institute, Christ opened another door for me to learn more about vision development. I was connected with an organization that was already a proven ministry, and my thinking was challenged even more. A member of our church worked for the Lutheran Service Organization, and he was asked to help build a team of people who could be used to develop their vision in Saginaw. Their goal was to continue their service in a better and bigger way, and I felt blessed to be recommended to work on this team. This was one of the greatest programs I had ever worked with.

I also had the privilege to take with me a few of my leaders to share in the work on different teams. We spent several meetings brainstorming the ideas put before us by the leaders of the Lutheran organization. We were instructed that the vision had to be written in sixteen words or less. We were very successful in the development of the vision and the mission. We learned so much in just seven meetings. We learned how to determine the marks of distinction of the organization that would set it apart from the rest. We learned how to remove the prison perception or negative outlook from the community through the power of media while casting vision. We learned how to sell our products as we developed them. We also learned how to identify the hiccups or the things causing the most problems in the community and how to create programs to help usher in change to remove the problem. This is simply done by putting in place positive programs and services that are missing in the community. I am so grateful to God because as He was planning the turnaround, He was certifying the vision for our church.

Confirmation for the Vision

At this point, the vision was truly confirmed as a vision from God that would last even after I was off the scene. These great leaders were truly part of the answer to the prayer my friend told me to pray. They awakened my mind to what it meant to have a clear vision that pointed to what God wanted to do through the ministry. Their teachings made me stop, think, and re-evaluate what I was doing as a pastor. They motivated me to dig deeper and inspired me to hear God speak. I was totally convinced that building a ministry to meet the needs of the whole person was God's direction for our church. All I needed at this point was the Scripture base for the vision. One day as I was sitting in my office, meditating on the vision and researching Scriptures, the Holy

Spirit led me to my vision Scripture and showed me how the Scripture worked together with the vision and mission of the church.

The Vision's Scripture Base

> Jesus grew in wisdom and stature and in favor with God and men. (Luke 2:52 NIV)

In the vision Scripture, there are four areas of growth describing how Jesus grew while He was on earth:

- "Wisdom" is intellectual growth, which is the development of the mind.
- "Stature" is physical growth, which is the development of the body.
- Favor with God" is spiritual growth, which is the development of the soul.
- "Favor with men" is social growth, which is the development of community.

The following quote is what He spoke to me for our church:

To build a ministry to meet the needs of the whole person through a process of intellectual, physical, spiritual, and social development, that together we might affect change in our church community and world.

To live the kind of life Christ wants us to live or to develop the kind of church He wants to build, these four growth patterns are necessary. They provide the balance we need as we grow to spiritual maturity.

I believe these pillars of growth provided balance to Jesus' life as He performed His mission.

God inspired me with the vision, mission, core values, outcome, and logo for the church from this Scripture. It was critically necessary for me to know how to break down this direction from God so I could articulate it to the congregation.

The Vision Statement

To build a ministry to meet the needs of the whole person.

The vision statement speaks to where we are going and what we plan to do. "To build" represents an action that will continue until the work is completed. "To build a ministry" speaks to specifically to what we are building so we don't lose focus. "To build a ministry for the whole person" speaks to the scope of our service as we minister to the basic needs of every person the Spirit sends to us.

The Mission Statement

Meeting needs through a process of intellectual, physical, spiritual, and social development.

The mission statement speaks to how we are going to make the vision become reality and the process we will use to measure success based on the intellectual, physical, spiritual, and social needs of the people. Our mission is to develop these four pillars in the heart of every believer God sends us. If these developments are not taking place, then we know our work is not in alignment with the vision. The mission pushes the vision in the direction it should be going.

Our Top Four Core Values

To meet the needs of the whole person, God revealed to me the mission pillars must become the top four core values of the church. Core values are the unbending principles we will not compromise. They help us become part of the vision as we focus on meeting the needs of the whole person. Everything we do must be covered by one of these values, or we cannot allow it to take place in the church. Our programs, ministries, events, and services—they all must be conducive to our purpose. The core values lead to spiritual maturity and protect the vision from being destroyed. These values will also protect the vision from being rerouted by those who think the church should be doing something different. A strong set of core values will guide a church along its way by providing principles to keep the members on track.

Our first core value is intellectual development: The development of the mind. We believe knowledge is power; therefore, we value learning, whether biblical or secular, because it constitutes the development of the intellect, motivating us to celebrate education, promote graduations, and encourage higher learning at all times.

Our second core value is physical development: The development of the body. We believe physical development prolongs life. We value caring for the body through physical exercise, aerobics, and walking. We also value healthy eating, dressing appropriately, and looking nice. We believe if a person can look good, he or she will feel good, resulting in a person doing well.

Our third core value is spiritual development: The development of the soul. We value worship, prayer, meditation, and quiet time with God. We believe through worship we gain power to live our day-to-day lives. Through our daily worship, devotion, and relationship with Him, the anointing of God is released in our lives. We believe all people need to have a close relationship with God so they are connected to a power greater than themselves.

Our fourth core value is social development: The development of community. We value community and believe the church is made up of the community in which it exists. It is what we do with each other that count among us. We believe every person needs healthy relationships because every person is important. We believe healthy relationships build healthy communities and healthy communities build healthy cities.

The Outcome

That, together, we might affect change in our community and world.

The outcome we expect to see is the entire church playing a part in bringing people to Christ and the church making a positive difference in the community. Church growth is about people working together to meet the needs of others, which results in more people being saved. God gives vision to fulfill one overall purpose in the church, and that purpose is to fulfill the Great Commission of Jesus Christ. When this is being done, change will automatically take place in our lives and in the lives of others. Our primary goal in all we do is to fulfill the Great Commission, as the Word teaches us.

Therefore go and make disciples of all nations, baptizing
them in the name of the Father and of the Son and of the
Holy Spirit, and teaching them to obey everything I have
commanded you. And surely I am with you always, to the
very end of the age. (Matt. 28:19–20 NIV)

The work of the vision and mission together will also result in people
praising God in the community and everywhere else. The results of vision will
be seen in the men and women affecting change in their communities by their
service and contributions. Together our work will open the eyes of the blind
by making them see the good Christ is doing through the church. Our work
is supposed to make people see and praise God. The Scripture says,

In the same way, let your light shine before men, that they
may see your good deeds and praise your Father in heaven.
(Matt. 5:16 NIV)

Vision helps us to let our lights shine before men. The light in us is seen
through what we do, not what we say. The people who will be affected by
our lights are not those on the inside of the church but those who are on the
outside. They are the ones who are watching to see what the church is going
to do. When they see the work of the church as it relates to community
development, they will be compelled to praise God for the work they see.
The work of the church has always been Christ's idea for changing lives in
the community. Christ's intent for the church is clear in this Scripture:

His intent was that now, through the church, the manifold
wisdom of God should be made known to the rulers and
authorities in the heavenly realms. (Eph. 3:10 NIV)

It is through the work we do together as a body of believers that God's wisdom is made known to the world. Working together describes people who are of one mind and serving on the same team. Again, Solomon explains teamwork best in the following verses:

> Two are better than one, because they have a good return for their work: If one falls down, his friend can help him up. But pity the man who falls and has no one to help him up! Also, if two lie down together, they will keep warm. But how can one keep warm alone? Though one may be overpowered, two can defend themselves. A cord of three strands is not quickly broken. (Eccles. 4:9–12 NIV)

Solomon shows clearly how effective two or more can be and what they can accomplish. We can get so much more done if people are willing to work together; this is the purpose of vision. Vision paints the picture so we can see what it looks like before it becomes a reality. Our passion to do the work will give birth to the hunger and energy that keeps us on course. People committed to work together in making the vision become reality will make up a cord of unity that is not quickly broken. People push the mission, and the mission pushes the vision, which results in changed people, a changed church, a changed community, and a changed world.

The Logo

NEW LIFE MINISTRIES

Now that the vision, mission, core values, and expected outcome have been made clear, I am able to paint a clear picture that captures the entire DNA of the church. This logo is a quick look at what the church is about and the reason it exists. We use this logo on everything we do: it is plastered on the walls of the church and is on every bulletin, CD, DVD, letterhead, and envelope. This logo represents a ministry for the whole person. The three crosses represent Jesus' death for the church. The cross being empty means He is no longer here but has gone back to the Father. The year represents when we came into being as a church. The arch represents the earth in which the church is to serve.

The four pillars represent the structure holding the church together. The outer edge houses the names of the four pillars, which are also the mission prerequisites used to determine everything we do as we fulfill the vision. Together they produce a clear picture of the vision, mission, and core values working together to produce the expected outcome of the overall vision for the church: to effect change in the church, community, and world.

The next four chapters of this book will present a deeper look at the vision pillars or core values as they stress the importance of the development for each pillar. I really believe they were given to us in Scripture to provide the balance we need in our lives and to keep us from capsizing in the ocean of life due to a lack of balance. I will also share the programs we use to put each of them into action.

Chapter 4

Intellectual Development

In this chapter, we will explore the importance of intellectual development in the body of Christ and how we can use it as motivation while we are preparing people for life on earth. The Bible teaches how Jesus' life on earth exemplified a ministry for the whole person. Intellectual development was part of this process. The Bible says,

> And Jesus grew in wisdom and stature, and in favor with God and men. (Luke 2:52 NIV)

The first clause of this verse says Jesus grew in wisdom. Several things come to mind when we refer to wisdom, and many traits are found under its umbrella describing Jesus' character. Wisdom suggests Jesus grew in understanding, knowledge, insight, intelligence, perception, and good judgment. I believe this is how God would have all of His children grow. I also believe Jesus grew in all of these attributes, which helped Him live a full and balanced life on earth. It is clear from Scripture how God wants us to model the life of Christ.

> Let this mind be in you, which was also in Christ Jesus.
> (Phil. 2:5 KJV)

From a spiritual sense, intellectual development is the development of the mind. This development works best when we spend time with God's Word and let it transform our lives. Transformation has a lot to do with what we practice and feed our minds on a daily basis. We are warned in Scripture not to feed on the entertainment of the world but rather to feed on the things of God. The Scripture teaches us to

> Do not conform any longer to the pattern of this world, but
> be transformed by the renewing of your mind. Then you will
> be able to test and approve what God's will is—his good,
> pleasing and perfect will. (Rom. 12:2 NIV)

Our intellect allows us to read and understand the meaning of the Scriptures and to apply what we have read to our lives. We must commit to God's Word if we are to have knowledge of how He wants us to live. After spending time with the Word, we must pray for wisdom to know how to use it. Wisdom is a gift from God to us. He gives it only to those who truly seek it and ask Him for it.

> If any of you lacks wisdom, he should ask God, who gives
> generously to all without finding fault, and it will be given to
> him. (James 1:5 NIV)

The goal of this chapter is to provide insight on how the people of God can benefit from knowledge and wisdom. If the church is going to move forward, it must find ways to educate the people of God and to reach the great minds of its family. We must also find ways to promote both spiritual and secular education because it takes both to complete the learning process. Secular education is there to help articulate the Word of God more effectively. Spiritual and secular knowledge increase the intellectual power of the church, while wisdom shows us how to use it. When people know what to do and how to do it, life becomes much easier to manage, and churches become much easier to grow. The Holy Spirit is seeking people who will let Him educate them in the ways of the kingdom so both the church and community can benefit. For the next few pages, I want to talk about intellectual development as it relates to the power of knowledge.

Knowledge Approves Us before God

So many times in life, we look to others for approval. If we want God's approval, we must look in the right direction—toward His Word. The Word of God provides all the knowledge and wisdom necessary to make good choices and to lead the kind of life pleasing to Him. God created us, and the Bible is our instructional manual. Through the Word of God, we are to be rebuked, corrected, and encouraged. Therefore, it is absolutely essential for every child of God to be engaged in the study of the Word. The Bible makes it plain whose approval we should seek, how to get it, and the benefits of having it, as seen in Scripture:

> Study to shew thyself approved unto God, a workman that needeth not to be ashamed, rightly dividing the word of truth. (2 Tim. 2:15 KJV)

If we are going to be approved by God, we must be willing to do the mental labor to make it happen. We must be willing to burn the midnight oil by reading and studying the Word of God. Studying the Word is different from reading the Word. Reading will familiarize you with the text, while studying will educate you in it. When studying, you take notes as you read, being sure to pay attention to punctuation marks so you can pause and reflect on what you have read. You will also need to look up Scripture references to see what else God is saying in other places in the Bible.

Studying is the starting point, and from there application can be made. We cannot be great communicators of the Word without studying it first. When we understand the Word and let it be our guide, it will equip us at every point of life. The Scriptures teach,

> The whole Bible was given to us by inspiration from God and is useful to teach us what is true and to make us realize what is wrong in our lives; it straightens us out and helps us do what is right. It is God's way of making us well prepared at every point, fully equipped to do good to everyone. (2 Tim. 3:16–17 TLB)

There are several life-changing truths standing out in these verses that will help us see and understand the effects of the Word when it is applied to our lives.

It Teaches Us What Is True

The Word of God shows us what is accurate—what is correct and incorrect. The only answer to Satan's lies is God's truth. The Word of God can expose every lie the enemy tells. I found out in my years of Christian experience that if you can't find Scripture supporting what you are about to do, then it may not be a good idea. The fact is, if God doesn't approve it, it doesn't matter who says it is all right. When we fail to learn God's Word through frequent studying, we open ourselves up to listening and accepting whatever anyone tells us, whether it comes from another faith or from people who misinterpret the Scriptures by taking God's Word out of context.

The Bible is the truth of God and will always remain the same. When we take the time to study God's Word and learn it for ourselves, we are better equipped to discern if doctrines from others are correct. Also, we will be better able to fight against the Devil's schemes:

> Put on the full armor of God so that you can take your stand against the devil's schemes. (Eph. 6:11 NIV)

> For the Lord gives wisdom, and from his mouth come knowledge and understanding. (Prov. 2:6 NIV)

It Shows Us What's Wrong in Our Lives

The Word reveals our errors and exposes our rebellions. It points out our mistakes; it shows us our faults and our inaccuracies; and it shows us who is wrong and who is right. The Word makes God's voice personal to us and challenges us in all our wrongdoings. It shows us what is wrong in our lives. This is critically important because we can't help others until we have ourselves under control. When we study God's Word, we can't help but to see how it speaks directly to us. Christ shows us through Scripture how we should live as Christians. When we compare the way we are actually living to the way Christ says we should live and the two don't match up, it's a clear warning we are doing something wrong. We need to examine our lives, seek to change our behavior, and start doing what is right so our lives may be pleasing to God.

It Straightens Us Out

The Word will not only show you what's wrong, but it will also straighten you out and make you see what you are doing wrong. It will show you how to correct your mistakes and how to fix what is broken. We receive knowledge through God's Word to help us correct the things currently afflicting our lives. We must be careful to let God's Word guide us and not ignore the instructions He gives us. By doing this, we can correct our errors and avoid leaning on our own understanding.

It Helps Us Do What Is Right

The Word will train you for the test of life. It trains you to live God's way. It will help you accomplish your goals for life. It helps you complete your task. The Word will help you love, forgive, and show mercy to others. Again the Scripture says,

> It is God's way of making us well prepared at every point, fully equipped to do good to everyone. (2 Tim. 3:17 TLB)

When God's Word is deeply rooted in our hearts, it is much easier for us to do what is right because it equips us and directs all aspects of our lives. If we don't invite Spirit into our lives every day, then we are refusing His guidance, which results in many life complications. When God is in the picture, life is simpler because He helps us make wiser decisions, which leads to a better outcome in everyday living.

Knowledge Reduces Stress in Life

I found out that one can work hard or one can work smart. The more you know about something, the easier it is for you to master it; the less you know, the harder it is. That's the way life is, and that's why we go to school and attend workshops and conferences as leaders to make the work easier for us. When thinking of ways to reduce stress in life, there are several stress busters to consider.

1. Learning to Trust God Is a Great Stress Buster

> Trust in the Lord with all your heart and lean not to your own understanding; in all your ways acknowledge him, and he will make your paths straight. (Prov. 3:5–6 NIV)

God has given us this conditional promise: He says if we trust in Him with all our hearts instead of depending on our own limited understanding and acknowledge Him in all we do, then He will make our paths straight. Trusting God will bring about success in your life—a success only God can produce. This Scripture tells us we should rely upon God when we have tough decisions to make. Stress in life can be reduced if we let Him take care of life's details. God specializes in the details of our lives. He wants us to give Him the areas in our lives that are problematic for us. If we are experiencing health concerns, job issues, parenting issues, clothing concerns, or worry about what we will eat, Christ wants us to give Him these areas of stress so He can work them out for us. He wants us to let Him deal with the details of our lives so we can focus on the work of the kingdom, according to the Word of God.

> But seek first his kingdom and his righteousness, and all these things will be given to you as well." (Matthew 6:33 NIV)

2. Developing Life Skills Is a Great Stress Buster

You can remove a lot of stress by learning the skills needed for a successful life. The Bible makes it plain, saying,

If the ax is dull and its edge unsharpened, more strength is needed but skill will bring success. (Eccles. 10:10 NIV)

Whatever you are trying to do in life, if the ax is dull, you will have to work harder to accomplish your goals. Sharpening your ax is recognizing where a problem exists and then acquiring the knowledge or skills to fix it or make it better. First you have to find the area where your ax is dull and then sharpen it by improving your skills.

Working in an area outside the bounds of your giftedness can cause unneeded stress in your life. You will expend too much energy trying to get yourself mentally prepared to do the job when it should come naturally. These are the times when you don't want to go to work and are tempted to just call in sick. You are naturally better prepared to do the work if you are gifted for the job.

There are many college students who want to drop out of school because they have picked the wrong major. The classes are tough and the tests are harder to pass because it's not their strength. They could have easily picked a major relevant to the gifts the Holy Spirit gave them to live their lives by, which would bring them joy as they pursued their education. If we would take the time to discover our gifts, talent, and abilities, we could transfer them into our dream jobs, resulting in us being fulfilled, because we are connected with the life God intended for us to live. This same scenario can be used for serving in church ministries. Sometimes people are asked to serve in ministry that is not in their area of giftedness. Working out of your own strength will only take you so far. If it's not your gifted area, you will skip, miss, and eventually stop working in the ministry. These actions will cause the ministry leader to be stressed and frustrated, not knowing if a worker is going to show up when it is time to serve.

3. Practicing Obedience to God's Promises Is a Great Stress Buster

Financial issues can be a source of stress. Knowledge of what the Word says and putting it into practice can help us get through those tough financial times in our lives. We need to put God first in our finances if we want to live stress free. The Word tells us,

> "Bring the whole tithe into the storehouse, that there may be food in my house. Test me in this," says the LORD Almighty, "and see if I will not throw open the floodgates of heaven and pour out so much blessing that there will not be room enough to store it. I will prevent pests from devouring your crops, and the vines in your fields will not drop their fruit before it is ripe," says the LORD Almighty. (Mal. 3:10–11 NIV)

What God promises in these verses is conditional and will keep us from financial ruin if we obey. We are instructed to bring the whole tithe—not part of it but the whole thing—to God. When we do so, He promises to open up the floodgates of heaven and pour out blessings into our lives, which will be protected from the things that cause us the most stress. Solomon says it this way:

> Honor the LORD with your wealth, with the first fruits of all your crops; then your barns will be filled to overflowing, and your vats will brim over with new wine. (Prov. 3:9–10 NIV)

This is another conditional promise from God. We are told to honor the Lord with our wealth (the first part), and our barns will be filled to overflowing. If we practice obedience to the Word of God, we can eliminate financial stress in our lives.

4. Determining What You Can Do Before You Do It Is a Great Stress Buster

> Suppose one of you wants to build a tower. Will he not first
> sit down and estimate the cost to see if he has enough money
> to complete it? (Luke 14:28 NIV)

Oftentimes we find ourselves making purchases we do not need because we think we need the latest gadget or top-of-the-line model. We get ourselves into financial trouble when we do not have the means to pay cash for our purchases and have to rely on credit cards. Many people have had to file for bankruptcy because of their heavy reliance on credit cards. They didn't bother to count up the cost, and they got in way over their heads financially. God does not want us to be a slave to our creditors. The Word tells us we are "lenders and not borrowers" (Deut. 15:6 NIV). We show ourselves as true disciples of God when we consult Him and His Word before we make financial decisions. I will share more about this in the financial program session of this chapter.

Knowledge Saves Us from Destruction

The Bible is very clear on what will happen if we fail to educate ourselves. It warns us in advance of the outcome:

> My people are destroyed for lack of knowledge. (Hosea 4:6 KJV)

So many times we blame others for what we do not have when it's really our fault. When we fail to educate ourselves, we bring harm upon ourselves and our community. What hurts us more than anything is what we don't know, which will sometimes affect the people around us.

In Hosea's days, the Lord held the leaders responsible for the people's lack of knowledge; today He tells people everywhere to teach others what they have been taught, according to the Great Commission,

> Therefore go and make disciples of all nations, baptizing them
> in the name of the Father and of the Son and of the Holy
> Spirit, and *teaching them to obey everything I have commanded*
> *you.* And surely I am with you always, to the very end of the
> age. (Matt. 28:19–20 NIV)

The secret to being saved from the destruction that comes from a lack of knowledge is to continue in the word God has given us. If we do, the Scripture promises we will be blessed.

> But the man who looks intently into the perfect law that
> gives freedom, and continues to do this, not forgetting what
> he has heard, but doing it—*he will be blessed in what he does.*
> (James 1:25 NIV)

Jesus had some powerful words for the Jews who believed in Him.

> If ye *continue in my word*, then are ye my disciples indeed;
> and ye shall *know the truth*, and the *truth shall make you free.*
> (John 8:31–32 NIV)

Jesus said if we continue in His Word, it will prove we are His disciples, and the Word will teach us the truth and knowing the truth will make us free. There are many ways to apply this Scripture to our lives, all of which will save us from being destroyed for a lack of knowledge. Other than knowing the truth about God, Christ, and the work of the Holy Spirit, there are other areas we must know the truth in to be made free.

I Must Know the Truth about Myself

To know is to have knowledge. It is only through persistent learning that we will know the truth. To know the truth about Christ is important. To know the truth about who we are and our strengths, gifts, talents, abilities, and personality is just as important for the sake of balance. Knowing you are not gifted for a certain job will keep you from applying, which saves you and the company from wasting time, energy, and resources. If you know a job doesn't suit your gifts, talents, abilities, or personality, then you should not apply for the job.

Some people search all over the world to find the truth about themselves. Some people even pay psychics thousands of dollars just to hear someone tell them about themselves or what their future supposedly holds. Others will try different lifestyles, religions, cults, and classes searching for the truth. What we sometimes fail to understand is to find out about ourselves, we have to consult with the Maker. When you purchase a car, it comes with an owner's manual telling you how the vehicle operates so you can operate the vehicle to its fullest. When you buy something that needs to be put together, you must read the directions from the manufacturer. Likewise, if we want to know about ourselves, we need to consult with God, the Creator of all mankind. The Bible says He knew us before we were formed in our mother's womb. This is before we were thought of by our parents.

> Before I formed you in the womb I knew you, before you were born I set you apart ... (Jeremiah 1:5 NIV)

If you don't know what you are supposed to be doing in this life, you need to check with God. When God made you, He had a purpose for you and gave you the tools to run your life on earth. Here are four Scriptures that prove God had something special in mind for us:

For we are God's *workmanship*, created in Christ Jesus *to do good works*, which *God prepared in advance* for us to do. (Eph. 2:10 NIV)

It is he who saved us and chose us for his *holy work* not because we deserved it but because *that was his plan long before the world began*—to show his love and kindness to us through Christ. (2 Tim. 1:9 TLB)

But God in his grace *chose me* even before I was born, and *called me to serve him*. (Gal. 1:15 GNB)

God has given each of you some *special abilities*; be sure to use them to help each other, passing on to others God's many kinds of blessings. (1 Peter 4:T10 LB)

I Must Know the Truth about People

Just knowing who is for you and against you will help you get along in life. To be able to detect harm that could come upon you by others is a good sense to have; it will protect you over the long haul. The Scripture makes it plain the danger of hanging with certain kind of people:

Do not be misled: "Bad company corrupts good character." (1 Cor. 15:33 NIV)

We have to love them, but they can't be our best friends. Knowledge of their character sets us free. When we use our knowledge in the correct way, it will set us free from the things that once held us in bondage. Sometimes it's hard to tell who they are, but if we have the Spirit of discernment, God will show us who they are. Once we know the difference, we must adjust our lives accordingly.

Wisdom Will Bless Us If We Pursue It

Life is better with wisdom, but wisdom and knowledge don't come automatically; they have to be sought after. It is something you have to want and be willing to go to the extreme to get. Moses put it this way:

> See, I have taught you decrees and laws as the Lord my God
> commanded me, so that you may follow them in the land you
> are entering to take possession of it. Observe them carefully,
> *for this will show your wisdom and understanding* to the nations,
> who will hear about all these decrees and say, "Surely this great
> nation is a wise and understanding people. (Deut. 4:5–6 NIV)

According to these verses, we pursue wisdom by our willingness to be taught and our commitment to obey what we are taught. In whatever we do, if we observe what we have been taught carefully, God's promise to help us stand against our enemies is guaranteed.

> For I will give you words and wisdom that none of your
> adversaries will be able to resist or contradict. (Luke 21:15 NIV)

This verse makes it clear nothing can match the wisdom God, gives and it cannot be denied by your adversaries or contradicted. This wisdom will start with the fear of God in our lives.

> The fear of the Lord is the beginning of wisdom: a good understanding have all they that do his commandment: His praise endureth forever. (Ps. 111: 10 NIV)

It is never too late to get wisdom, and by no means will God keep it from us, but it does come with a price. You must want to please God with your life. Doing this produces tremendous results. The questions for a church to answer are: "What kind of educational programs do we need to have in place to make this happen? Do we see the vision for it? Can we write the vision on paper? Can it be done? How long will it take, and when will we begin? Do we have the wisdom, knowledge, and understanding to make it happen?"

> Now that you know these things, you will be blessed if you do them. (John 13:17 NIV)

> But be ye doers of the word, and not hearers only, deceiving your own selves. (James 1:22 KJV)

Intellectual Development Programs

The vision would not be complete without programs to make it happen. I will elaborate on a few of these God-given programs, with the hope of being a blessing to someone who is truly seeking educational programs to consider as they plan their studying curriculum.

Midweek Bible Study

A few years back, I started a simple Bible study that affected more lives than any study I have taught. This program is called "Biblical

Application through Scripture Memorization." In this program, there are a few areas of concentrated focus called "Discovery."

Discover the Promise

People usually respond to rewards and what benefits them. If I can show you the rewards behind what I am teaching from the Word of God, you will be more driven to memorize what the Word says. The reward is what makes you want to continue, and after you receive the reward, you will be more motivated to memorize even more Scripture.

Discover the Requirement

Wherever you find a conditional promise in Scripture, you will also find a requirement you must fulfill to receive the blessing. Most people want the blessings, but they do not want the requirement. Obedience to the Word of God is the secret to receiving the promise God made to us.

Discover the Evaluation

Here you complete a personal assessment to determine whether you are in alignment with the Word. First, you study the promise, and then you evaluate your behavior against the requirements and determine why you are blessed or why you are not being blessed.

Discover the Prayer

After you have discovered the promise and fulfilled the requirement, you can pray back to God what He promised in the Scripture. God wants us to pray back to Him what He said to us. When you pray His promises, you will never find yourself wondering about what to pray. God's promises can be applied to every area of our life. It's as simple as this: "God, You said if I do this, You will do that. I have done what You told me to do."

The most fascinating thing I heard when I started teaching this God-given program was, "Pastor, I have never in all my Christian life learned and memorized so many Scriptures." I taught one Bible verse a week for about six months. My hope was for the members to learn twenty to twenty-five Scriptures in a six-month period. During this time, the church studied the promises from the Word of God relating to faith, prosperity, salvation, and healing and Scriptures that revealed the character traits of God so we might know Him better. For each Scripture, I did my best to explain it in a way that would make them not only understand, but would also produce a hunger in them to memorize it.

Again, let's review the steps. First, I teach them the promise, then the requirement to receive the promise, and then how to evaluate their lives based on both the promise and the requirement. Finally, they learn how to pray those Scriptures into their lives and the lives of others. This study is designed to help the church parishioners analyze if they are hearing what God speaks to them and if they are doing the things necessary to receive the promises. For the sake of clarity, here is an example of one lesson I taught.

Lesson One

The Scripture to Remember

He who conceals his sins does not prosper, but whoever confesses and renounces them finds mercy. (Prov. 28:13 NIV)

The word *conceal* means to hide or cover up your sin, with the hope that no one will find out about it. It means to not admit to your faults. You can hide and hide, and maybe you will get away with them for a while, but eventually you will finally cross the line with God. When you cross the line with God, no one can help you. Unconfessed sins will separate you from Him, according to the Word:

> But your iniquities have separated you from your God; your sins have hidden his face from you, so that he will not hear. (Isa. 59:2 NIV)

For this information, the goal is to show the danger of unconfessed sins and the damage they can do if they continue to live in a person's heart. I want people to see how it will stop them from prospering and how it will wear them down over the long haul if they don't do something about it. At this point, I need them to really feel the painful effects of sin in hopes of bringing them closer to God.

The Promise: I Can Find Mercy with God

Mercy is getting another chance when you don't deserve it. Mercy is an opportunity to learn from your past. What good is a mistake if it does not teach you something? Mercy is a chance to analyze your mistakes and make adjustments so they don't happen again. God's promise of mercy is available to us. If we do the right thing, we can find mercy with God to help us come out of sin. The end of the verse says I can find mercy. I want people to see, according to the study verse, that mercy is there to help when they are ready to confess, in hopes they want to do something about their sin. At this point, I issue them a challenge by showing them the power to be forgiven is in their hand, and it will happen if they fulfill two requirements.

Requirement 1—Confess Your Sin

To confess your sin is to tell the truth, plead guilty, admit you have done wrong, and get it out. By confessing your sin, you will find mercy. Confession results in God's forgiveness.

Requirement 2—Renounce Your Sin

To renounce your sin is to profess you are finished with the sin. You must dismiss it from your life by walking away from it—refusing, rejecting, denying, and forsaking it. Then you will find mercy and forgiveness. If you want mercy from God, you must renounce your sin. We can make our mouths say anything, but renunciation is confession in action. This is what the Bible says:

> If we confess our sins, he is faithful and just and will forgive us our sins and purify us from all unrighteousness. (1 John 1:9 NIV)

At this point, I stress to them that if they do their part, God will do His part. Through His mercy, their lives can be restored because God will forgive and purify them from all unrighteousness.

The Evaluation

This is to study and evaluate your life according to the Scripture to see if you're ready for the blessings; to see if you have really confessed and renounced your sin. I want the people to measure their lives by the promise and its requirements to see where they stand with God. If they do not like what they see, they can correct their position and do something about it.

The Prayer

After the evaluation, we will know what to pray about. We can thank Him for keeping us or ask Him to fix us by telling Him what we are willing to do on our part. Now we pray the Scripture into our lives. An example: "Dear Jesus, today I confess my sins to You, and I am willing to walk away from them. I thank You for the mercy You have shown me by giving me another chance. In Jesus' name I pray, amen." This program was used as an educational tool for the Wolverine State Baptist Congress of Christian Education for two years from 2010 till 2012. *Please read the dean's comments in appendix I.*

Financial Program

Budgets Made Simple: Learning My Finances

As part of promoting intellectual development, I teach a class titled "Budget Made Simple: Learning My Finances." In this class, I present a step-by-step self-help guide to budgeting finances. The Lord has fulfilled a dream in my life to help my church members overcome financial burdens in their personal lives. This class helped those who took it to better manage their day-to-day finances in a way that enhanced both themselves and the work of the kingdom of God.

In my twenty-seven years of pastoring, I have seen people who wanted to honor God with their lives related to giving, but their lives were already overburdened with debt. To give tithes and offerings would only add to the burden. The budget class helped ease the stress by teaching them how to count up the cost, to think things over before spending (whether large or small amounts), and the importance of not spending if they didn't have to so they could cut down on the financial waste. A great lesson on this can be learned from Scripture.

> Suppose one of you wants to build a tower. Will he not first
> sit down and estimate the cost to see if he has enough money
> to complete it? (Luke 14:28 NIV)

This verse can be applied to many things—mainly finances. It's easy to count up the cost; we just need to take the time to do the math. In my class, I teach the simple things that need to take place before spending. For instance, look at what you want to buy, determine how much you can afford to spend, and then compare it with the income you currently have after paying your debt to see if you have enough. Another way to do this is to take a look at each week to see what week you will have enough cash available to take on another payment without cutting out anything else important, including your tithes to God. If you cannot find a place to pay for your desired purchase, then you have your answer.

This budget class will keep you from getting in debt or it will show you how to get out of debt. It's the simple things we do that provide us with financial freedom. This class will teach anyone whose finances are out of control how to bring stability through the Word of God. It reminds me of the story of Moses leading the people of God in Exodus 15. When they reached the place called Marah, the people were thirsty but the water was bitter. God told Moses to pick up a certain stick and throw it into the water, and as a result, the water turned sweet. My point is this: most of the time, what we need to help people is actually right in front of us; we just need God to specifically show us where. The wisdom from this class teaches the people how to prepare financially for the future, as the Scripture tells us,

The wise man saves for the future, but the foolish man spends whatever he gets. (Prov. 21:20 TLB)

The Scripture tells us we should be more responsible by saving our money. When we save, we can have something for unexpected expenses that may arise. Savers rarely experience debt or have to file for bankruptcy. I believe, unless pastors are seeking ways to teach their members financial stability, we will always pressure them to give what they really don't have or to give against their will. It is to no advantage to them or the church if we operate under these circumstances. God honors a cheerful giver. If the church is to be financially secured, it must start with its members. Just as we teach people about God, salvation, heaven, hell, how to build relationships, and so on, we need to teach them about financial stability. It will do all leaders good to ask God to help them develop a financial program to teach the members in their churches who are suffering with financial matters.

Chapter 5

Physical Development

hapter 5 will cover the importance of developing the physical body. I feel the information is essential to understanding the care the body needs to operate on a day-to-day basis. The more we understand our bodies, the better we can care for them. According to our vision Scripture, reference is given to this development.

> And Jesus grew in wisdom and *stature*, and in favor with God and men." (Luke 2:52 NIV)

I see "growing in stature" as physical growth, which is not to be taken lightly. Physical growth has considerable value in the area where Jesus grew. It is made plain in Scripture the value it holds, even though it's not the most important part of human development. Paul says,

For physical training is of some value, but godliness has value for all things, holding promise for both the present life and the life to come. (1 Tim. 4:8 NIV)

The most emphasis in this verse is placed on the spiritual. We know spiritual development is of paramount value, but we must not overlook the part physical development plays in maintaining our stay on earth. Paul says it has "some value," which makes all the difference for living. My hope is that the readers see the importance of this physical development idea and commit themselves to do all they can to improve their quality of life.

I believe physical development is something Christ wants all of us to be concerned about because of its connection with life. This development has a lot to do with the outcome of our families when it comes to recreation. It will determine the effectiveness of our physical connection with one another. It has a lot to do with our jobs; a lack of physical fitness can affect our jobs, causing us to not be able to work and produce as we were hired to do. A lack of this development will also affect our work for Christ, because no matter how gifted we are, if we are not in shape to serve Him, then we are defeating the purpose He instilled in us, causing us to miss out on the joy of active service. I could name several reasons why physical development is so important, but there are three that stand out as more important than the others.

The First Reason: Our Bodies Don't Belong to Us

Our bodies belong to the one who made them. The Bible declares, "Everything in this world belongs to God."

The earth is the Lord's, and everything in it, the world, and all who live in it. (Ps. 24:1 NIV)

Do you not know that your body is a temple of the Holy
Spirit, who is in you, whom you have received from God? You
are not your own. (1 Cor. 6:19 NIV)

Just thinking about to whom the body belongs should make us go
the extra miles to care for it. Knowing that we are caretakers of another
man's property should also make us more serious about caring for the
body. The Bible teaches that we all will one day give an account for the
investment God made in us.

So then, each of us will give an account of himself to God.
(Rom. 14:12 NIV)

Therefore, as managers we must be good stewards of God's investment
so He can be proud of us when He call us to accountability.

The Second Reason: We're Not the Only One Living in It

According to the Word of God, the Holy Spirit lives in us. God has
reserved our bodies to be a place for His Holy Spirit to dwell:

Don't you know that you yourselves are God's temple and
that God's Spirit lives in you? (1 Cor. 3:16 NIV)

Anytime living quarters are shared with another, each party must
be mindful of how they live and conduct themselves. If I am the only
one living there, I can get away with more than I can with another.
However, I must respect the other person and be careful to not crowd
him out or force him to move out by the things I do and entertain.
For example, it's hard for a nonsmoker to live in the same house with a
smoker or a nondrinker with a drinker.

For the sake of preserving a place for the Holy Spirit to live, Paul places heavy emphasis on the repercussions that follow defiling or polluting the space the Holy Spirit is to occupy.

If any man defiles the temple of God, him shall God destroy; for the temple of God is holy, which temple ye are. (1 Cor. 3:17 KJV)

To violate this warning is a set up for destruction; God will permit our own actions to overwhelm us and destroy us. The things we think are good for us are the very things most likely to corrode the body. The Bible warns us of worldly pleasures that could defile the temple and tells us how to protect ourselves from them in this verse:

Do not conform any longer to the pattern of this world, but be transformed by the renewing of your mind. Then you will be able to test and approve what God's will is—his good, pleasing and perfect will. (Rom. 12:2 NIV)

The only way to protect ourselves from what the world has to offer is to feed our minds with God's Word and allow His truth to transform us. When we allow the world to squeeze us into its grip, our minds become reshaped by the world's thinking, causing us to respond to what the world has to offer. I believe one of the world's most enticing presentations to get us to defile the body is through sexual sin. Paul made the results of this sin very clear when he said these words:

Flee from sexual immorality. All other sins a man commits are outside his body, but he who sins sexually sins against his own body. (1 Cor. 6:18 NIV)

Paul warns people to run from sexual sin because of the effects it can have on a person's life. Sexual sin affects you differently than any other sin. Sex can bring about so much pain if it's not used as God intended. Sex was meant for marriage, and it has a way of affecting a person's mind when he or she engages in it otherwise; it is a powerful force designed to unite two people into one. The Word of God shows us the powerful effects of sexual activities.

Do you not know that he who unites himself with a prostitute is one with her in body? For it is said, "The two will become one flesh. (1Cor. 6:16 NIV)

According to this verse, when two people have sex, they become one. This is startling! It suggests to me that the more people we have sex with, the more people we become one with, dividing our bodies into many directions, increasing our chances of attracting sexually transmitted diseases that are serious threats to life. People can avoid the tragedy that can follow sex by focusing on these two ideas: our bodies are not our own, and we are not the only one living in it. One day we will have to give an account of how we treated our bodies.

The Third Reason: Because God Cares about Our Bodies

John gives some very encouraging words to motivate us to care for our bodies and to develop a healthy lifestyle, resulting in prolonged life and longevity in ministry.

Dear friend, I am praying that all is well with you and that your body is as healthy as I know your soul is. (3 John 1:2 TLB)

So many times people put all their emphasis on spiritual development, as if there are no other parts of growth. It's not good enough to read the Word and shout on Sundays and then mistreat the body the rest of the week. We need to minister to our bodies just as we minister to our souls. It is God's will for His people to be of good health. God wants us to enjoy a healthy life, which will not take place unless we do something to make it happen. We must care for our physical bodies just as we care for our spiritual beings.

Jesus is concerned about both. When Jesus was tempted by the devil to turn stones into bread to feed Himself He made God's Word very clear, saying these words:

It is written, Man shall not live by bread alone, but by every word that proceedeth out of the mouth of God. (Matt 4:4 KJV)

This is a message for the world today. We need both bread and Word to live this life. Jesus said we shall not live by bread alone or by Word alone. As a people, we must manage our lives in both areas to ensure we are being nourished as Jesus was nourished. With this in mind, I want to expound on a few important factors I believe are essential for the development of the physical man. These factors are rest, dieting, exercise, personal appearance, preventive care defense, and a few physical development programs we use to put our vision into action.

The Need for Proper Rest

One thing people suffer from most in today's world is a lack of rest. We involve ourselves in so much that we become exhausted. We are so busy doing what we feel is important that we sometimes forget what really is important. I know for a fact pastors are often guilty of not getting proper rest. Many times I have found myself planning work in my mind while on vacation, knowing the purpose of my vacation is to rest my mind.

Sometimes we are not good at managing our personal lives, and as a result, we don't get the rest we need. There have been times when I carried my work to bed with me, causing my mind to continue processing when I should be sleeping, robbing me of the deep sleep I need to function the next day. I really believe bad habits like these and other work-rest imbalances have caused many people to be sick, because after a while it breaks down their immune systems.

When I think about it, the first things doctors tell us when we are not feeling well is to get plenty of rest, along with the medication they prescribe. Without proper rest, we cannot effectively serve God, nor can we live our lives effectively. We need rested minds just for everyday living. The choices we make for our families, our work, and our personal lives seriously depend on proper rest. One thing I learned in life is not to make major decisions when tired. I admit this has not always been the case. I remember days when I made decisions while I was tired, and things didn't come out right.

Many times I tried to read my Bible while I was tired, and all I did was reread the same verses over and over. I discovered the best time to read my Bible is early in the morning after I wake up from a good night's sleep. It allows me to lock in most of what I read; you can understand God better after a good night's rest. All through Scripture, we see signs of men talking to God or doing great things for Him early in the morning, which suggests to me these men got their rest. There are many Scriptures speaking to this:

Early the next morning Abraham got up and saddled his
donkey. He took with him two of his servants and his son
Isaac. When he had cut enough wood for the burnt offering, he
set out for the place God had told him about. (Gen. 22:3 NIV)

And the Lord said unto Moses, Rise up early in the morning, and stand before Pharaoh, and say unto him, Thus saith the Lord God of the Hebrews, Let my people go, that they may serve me. (Ex. 9:13 NIV)

And Moses wrote all the words of the Lord, and rose up early in the morning, and builded an altar under the hill, and twelve pillars, according to the twelve tribes of Israel. (Ex. 24:4 NIV)

[David said]: O God, thou art my God; early will I seek thee: my soul thirsteth for thee, O satisfy us early with thy mercy; that we may rejoice and be glad all our days. (Ps. 90:14 KJV)

And all the people came early in the morning to him in the temple, for to hear him. (Luke 21:38 KJV)

And early in the morning he came again into the temple, and all the people came unto him; and he sat down, and taught them. (John 8:2 KJV)

All of these Scriptures suggest rest is important to doing the will of God, and it must be at the top of our daily lives. Not only is getting up early in the morning the best time to hear God speak, but it's also the best time to think and plan your day before your mind gets distracted with other things. According to the next Scripture, it is clear that every moving creature needs rest at some point.

Six days do your work, but on the seventh day do not work, so that your ox and your donkey may rest and the slave born in your household, and the alien as well, may be refreshed. (Ex. 23:12 NIV)

Rest is the time to get rejuvenated. It has a way of recharging the body for maximum performance, in our families as well as in our ministries. Jesus often emphasized rest to His followers after being so busy working with the people:

> Then, because so many people were coming and going that
> they did not even have a chance to eat, he said to them,
> "Come with me by yourselves to a quiet place and get some
> rest." So they went away by themselves in a boat to a solitary
> place. (Mark 6:31–32 NIV)

Good rest is essential in the development of man. It makes life much easier in many aspects. Getting proper rest gives you more energy for service and life without feeling overwhelmed and stressed. It is always to our advantage to know when to pull away from the work to rest, which allows ministry and life to continue in a compelling way.

The Need for Proper Diet

Dieting is a subject I believe all churches should make part of their ministry because it can help people in so many ways. In our churches, we have people who are suffering from obesity and other weight-related problems affecting their health in life-threatening ways, and we must find ways to help them. I believe we can make application with this from what Paul says,

> [God] His intent was that now, through the church, the
> manifold wisdom of God should be made known to the rulers
> and authorities in the heavenly realms. (Eph. 3:10 NIV)

Through the church, the wisdom of God should be made known. If the church is a ministry for the whole person, dieting and proper eating habits cannot be ignored. Many times we avoid issues we feel will offend people who have the problem. We are more inclined to talk about the effects of certain sin but shy away from the effects of obesity. If we teach it and build effective health programs, people won't be so intimidated.

I have learned over the years what we eat and how we feel have a lot to do with our performance throughout the course of each day. Our physical development works hand-in-hand with our intellectual development. What I feed my body will affect my learning ability. Not eating enough can interfere with learning just as much as overeating can. People can't process information properly if they are hungry; neither can they process it if they are stuffed or just eating the wrong food. Our health is directly affected by what we put into our bodies. Certain foods we consume could cause heart disease, diabetes, high blood pressure, and other major illnesses.

To develop physically, we must avoid overindulging in unhealthy foods. A good illustration for people who care for their diets is recorded in the first chapter of Daniel. The king inquired about Daniel and the three Hebrew boys, and he wanted them to be trained to serve in his kingdom. The king made it clear what kind of men he was looking for.

> One day the king ordered Ashkenazi, his highest palace
> official, to choose some young men from the royal family of
> Judah and from other leading Jewish families. The king said,
> "They must be healthy, handsome, smart, wise, educated, and
> fit to serve in the royal palace. Teach them how to speak and
> write our language." (Dan. 1:3–4 CEV)

If the king expected servants to meet all of these requirements to serve in his palace, shouldn't we be willing to do this and more for God, as His servants? Shouldn't we want to be healthy, good-looking, smart, wise, educated, and fit to serve? His emphasis was on physical, intellectual, and social development. It takes sacrifice to produce this kind of living. To produce the results he wanted, the king had his own diet plan consisting of meat and wine. But Daniel had a problem with it.

> But Daniel resolved not to defile himself with the royal
> food and wine, and he asked the chief official for permission
> not to defile himself in this manner. Now God had caused
> the official to show favor and sympathy to Daniel, but the
> official told Daniel, "I am afraid of my lord the king, who has
> assigned your food and drink. *Why should he see you looking
> worse than the other young men your age?* The king would then
> have my head because of you. (Dan. 1:8–10 NIV)

Daniel was not willing to break his diet. He was determined to say no even if it cost him his life. Like Daniel, we have to know when to say no to eating certain food and eat only what is healthy for us. Daniel was willing to go on a ten-day diet to prove his way was better than the king's way when it came to his health. He begged for a chance to prove it.

> "Please test your servants for ten days: Give us nothing but
> vegetables to eat and water to drink. Then compare our
> appearance with that of the young men who eat the royal food,
> and treat your servants in accordance with what you see." So he
> agreed to this and tested them for ten days. At the end of the

ten days they looked healthier and better nourished than any of the young men who ate the royal food. (Dan. 1:12–15 NIV)

When the king interviewed the young men, he found there was no one in the kingdom like them. There is enough in the next few verses to motivate anybody to improve their eating habits.

At the end of the time set by the king to bring them in, the chief official presented them to Nebuchadnezzar. The king talked with them, and he found none equal to Daniel, Hananiah, Mishael and Azariah; so they entered the king's service. In every matter of wisdom and understanding about which the king questioned them, he found them ten times better than all the magicians and enchanters in his whole kingdom. (Dan. 1:18–20 NIV)

Just by eating the right foods, they stood out among their peers. The Bible says there were none equal to them when it came to wisdom and understanding. They looked healthier and better nourished than the rest, and the king found them to be ten times better all because of the choices they made about their diet and their commitment to not give in to the requests of others. Just like everything else, the power to be successful lies in your commitment. The difference between healthy living and unhealthy living is in your commitment. Too many times when we make resolutions to eat right, we do well for a while but then we fall off the wagon because we flirt with our commitment. When it comes to physical development, let us encourage one another to live healthier lives as part of our ministry.

The Need for Proper Exercise

Being active is a key aspect of developing physically. Regular exercise encourages the body to respond at a faster rate. Our healing, thinking, reaction time, and endurance will greatly improve with regular exercise. It increases your ability to lose weight by boosting your metabolism, which causes you to burn calories and helps your body burn fat faster. We learn these things as we live. The older we get, the more we think about health and exercise.

When I was in my twenties, I never thought about walking for health like I do now; life experiences brought about this change. My wife, Linda, and I set a goal to walk three miles three times a week for health sustainability, and we feel great all week long. Regular exercise makes you physically and mentally healthier. It tones up your body and makes your skin look healthier and younger, which gives you a sense of self-motivation. It helps you to think clearly, it increases your energy level, and it also helps you to sleep better.

When you get regular exercise, your immune system is strengthened, which causes your body to fight off sickness and disease better. If your immune system is strong, you will not fall ill easily, and if you should, you will recover at a faster rate. No one can do this for you; it is our duty to keep ourselves physically fit. Living unhealthy is risky, if you do it long enough it will work against you. Life has already proven to us when people look good and feel good they are more eager to do good.

A few years ago, I had the privilege of working with a medical doctor who was a member of our church and a leader in one of our community development programs. At a city council meeting, she spoke on behalf of our mission, seeking permission to build a park. She was moved to share with us concerning the health condition of Saginaw and its citizen. She informed us that

Almost thirty-four percent (33.8 percent) of Saginaw's adults are obese. Another 35.3 percent are overweight. That means 69.1 percent of Saginaw's adults are overweight or obese.[4]

In addition to this information, she went on to say, "Some of the

---

4   www.mich.gov/documents/mdch/overweight_obesty_michigan_-_2009_287986_7.pdf.

citizens of Saginaw are plagued by the epidemics of obesity, diabetes, heart disease, high blood pressure, and arthritis." She further stated that obesity causes serious health problems, which decreases the quality of life, how long you live, and how well you feel. Obesity causes arthritis, high blood pressure, high cholesterol, asthma, coronary artery disease, strokes, heart attacks, diabetes, certain cancers, liver and gallbladder disease, sleep apnea, and respiratory problems. Obesity can cause poor life satisfaction, poor general health, poor physical health, poor mental health, and activity limitations. Yet she declared, "There are many people who could prevent or postpone premature death and disability through exercise."

She pointed out the benefits of exercise, which include lowering your risk of premature death; increasing your life expectancy; decreasing the rate of heart attacks, strokes, high cholesterol, high blood pressure, diabetes, and breast, pancreatic, and intestinal cancers; decreasing fatigue; increasing weight loss; and decreasing gallbladder disease and general disability. Exercise prolongs an elderly person's ability to be self-sufficient. It improves thinking processes, delays memory loss, decreases stress, anxiety, and depression, and improves the physical and psychological quality of life. I think this is enough information to make all people rethink how they care for the health of their physical body. When I heard it, I was moved instantly to start thinking about improving the quality of my personal life, and I hope it makes you react the same way.

The Need for a Good Personal Appearance

Personal appearance is also a necessary part of physical development. We use different grooming methods to maintain and improve our outward appearance. For this very purpose, people fill barber and beauty shops weekly. They stock their homes with cologne and perfume, fill makeup shops, and buy expensive jewelry. All of this is done to make a person feel good about his or her self. I really believe when a person's self-esteem is heightened, he or she feels he or she can accomplish the impossible.

Personal appearance has always played a part in human existence. It played a big part with many great men of the Bible who were selected to do special work in society. For example, in the first chapter of Daniel, the king chose Daniel and his friends to work in his palace and specified how they must look. When Samuel was about to crown Jesse's son Eliab to be the next king of Israel, thinking he was the Lord's anointed by virtue of his looks, the Lord said to him,

> Do not consider his appearance or his height, for I have rejected him. The Lord does not look at the things man looks at and think is important. Man looks at the outward appearance, but the Lord looks at the heart. (1 Sam. 16:7 NIV)

People today still value personal appearance. When it comes to hiring employees, businesses highly consider the outward appearance. They are not quick to hire people who don't value personal grooming because of the negative effect it could have on the image and production of the company. I believe many people have been rejected for jobs because of wearing the wrong clothes for the interview. Sagging pants or dirty clothing will not compel an employer to invest in you. Again, it is my firm belief that when people look good, they will feel good, which results in them doing well.

Preventative Care Defense

Preventative care defense is what we do to protect our bodies from sickness and disease. It plays a major role in developing physically. There are certain things required to keep the body healthy, such as seeing a doctor and/or dentist regularly. Regular doctor visits, eating right, and resting are forms of preventative care. There are also things we should stay away from to avoid putting our bodies at risk, like street drugs, prescription drug abuse, alcohol, and cigarettes, just to name a few. When we look at God's investment in making us His masterpiece of all creation, we should want to protect it.

> For you created my inmost being; you knit me together in my mother's womb. I praise you because I am fearfully and wonderfully made; your works are wonderful, I know that full well. My frame was not hidden from you when I was made in the secret place, when I was woven together in the depths of the earth. (Ps. 139:13–15 NIV)

God put so much into creating us, and it's our responsibility to take care of what He created. He has given us doctors for every part of our body so we can live a life of wellness, but it's up to us to make the appointment. The body doesn't break down all of a sudden; we always get warning signs to alert us something is wrong. When this happens, we need to go see the doctor and not pretend to be one.

As I write this chapter, I have a parishioner in the hospital who failed to get regular checkups from his doctor. As he was about his daily duties, making a living for his family, he felt his eyesight weakening. He drove himself to the hospital, and they admitted him. They discovered his sugar level was at 1,100. They got it down to 350 and it went back up to over 500. The doctors worked hard to save him from going into a coma, and as a blessing to him after being in the hospital for five days they were able to get his sugar level back in normal range. Again, God gave us doctors to care for our health.

Trust in the LORD with all your heart and lean not on your own understanding; in all your ways acknowledge him, and he will make your paths straight. Do not be wise in your own eyes; fear the LORD and shun evil. This will bring health to your body and nourishment to your bones. (Prov. 3:5–8 NIV)

Physical Development Programs

"Healthy Is Wealthy" Fitness Programs

We believe living healthy is living wealthy. If one can possess good health, one possesses the best quality of life. Therefore, there are several programs we do to ensure good health for the church and the community.

Aerobics/Exercise Program

In preparation for this program, I conducted a survey with 111 people in a Bible study with certain questions about health. One question was, "Do you exercise more than twice a week?" Forty-two out of 111 said they exercised more than twice a week, leaving 69 who didn't do any kind of exercise. These numbers spoke volumes to our church. The stats showed us how far off track we were for a healthy membership. They also showed us how current we were with the vision to build a ministry for the whole person.

After getting the facts, we cast the vision for a healthy-is- wealthy fitness program. We began to seek information on how we could put it into action. The Holy Spirit saw our concerns and connected us with an aerobics instructor in the community who had access to one of the greatest exercise rooms in town who was looking for someone to partner with in a fitness program. She provided us with a nurse to work with us in keeping records of weight and inches lost. She leads the group in quality prerecorded exercise videos that produce good results in the lives of the participants.

This program was God-sent; the timing was perfect, and the people bought into the idea. We had thirty people from the church to enroll in a ten-week exercise drive. Our goal was to empower them through exercise to keep them physically fit. Motivating them to get involved in this fitness program, we taught them two important things about life as it relates to mortality and morbidity. Our focus was on how exercise can increase the length of life (mortality) and the quality of life (morbidity). Just knowing this information is a motivating factor that will move people to get involved and save many lives. It's amazing how vision makes things come together and connect you with people who can help you make it happen. I discovered some vital information concerning the benefits of aerobics that can be found in *appendix II.*

Walking for Health

We promote health in our church just as we promote worship, Bible study, fellowship, and everything else. Since our church is organized around the life-development groups, each leader is required to stress the "Walking for Health" program within his or her group. The group leaders encourage their classes to meet together twice a week and walk as they build relationships with each other. This program is good for singles and married couples who are walking and sharing their lives together. I discovered some vital information concerning the benefits of walking, which can be found in *appendix III.*

Nutrition Program

Once a year, our goal is to host a comprehensive nutrition workshop to help our members and the community understand the value of healthy food and the importance of knowing how to use it to their advantage. In our health survey, we asked two more questions concerning eating and weight. The first question was, "Do you eat healthy every day?" Thirty-four out of 111 said they ate healthy, leaving 77 who didn't eat healthy. The next question was, "Are you overweight?" Eighty-seven out of 111 said they were overweight, leaving 24 who were not overweight. What do these numbers say to you? They say to me that my membership at large is not healthy, and something needs to be done about getting them on the right track.

I really think we sometimes forget food is supposed to be used to nourish our bodies. Most of us don't seem to realize there is more to eating than just filling our stomachs. What we eat is connected with our lives, and it will determine if we are healthy or unhealthy. Our bodies depend on us eating the right food so they can perform at an optimal level.

I remember when I used to have three tacos and a small can of pork and beans as an entrée, and my weight was never over 175 pounds. Then one day something happened; I was eating my tacos and beans, and I couldn't get enough. I kept on eating until I had consumed seven tacos and a small can of beans. On this day, I actually felt my stomach stretch. Those seven tacos and beans blew my stomach up. Afterward I could no longer eat three tacos and a small can of beans; I had to have more. I found out the more I ate, the bigger I stretched my stomach, and it took more food to satisfy me. I thought if I could just stop eating so much, everything would go back to normal, but I found out quickly that changing my eating habits was not easy. Once things get out of hand, you need a process to follow to put food back into perspective.

As I developed the vision God had given me for the church, I thought, *How can I teach a whole-person vision unless I can be an example of physical development as it relates to nutrition and good health myself?* I spoke with my wife about it, and we decided we would promote good health to the congregation by working on ourselves first and then encouraging the members to follow our lead. We took a diet plan we had heard about called the cabbage diet plan to help us get back on track with our weight and eating habits.[5] For the sake of teaching and giving it purpose, we called it the prayer diet fast.

The Prayer Diet Fast

This plan consisted of seven days of eating a variety of vegetables and fruit but very little meat and no bread. We added two things to make it fit our vision: prayer and Daniel's idea of the diet he requested the king to let him and his friends go on (ten days of nothing but vegetables and water). Our prayer focus was on developing the four pillars of the church in our lives: intellectual, physical, spiritual, and social development.

When Daniel and his friends completed their ten days, the king said they looked healthier and better nourished than any of the young men who ate the royal food. The text also says,

> "In every matter of wisdom and understanding about which
> the king questioned them, he found them ten times better
> than all the magicians and enchanters in his whole kingdom."
> Dan. 1:20 (NIV)

We encouraged our members to try it for seven days with a focus on the pillars we used to meet the needs of the whole person. After the seven days, we went back to our normal lifestyle but were careful about we ate. We had to try it first so we would know what the diet was like

---

5   The cabbage diet plan can be found at www.cabbage-soup-diet.com.

and what to expect so we could encourage the members who would follow the plan. We asked them to try the prayer diet fast with a prayer focus of the vision pillars by making it personal and asking God to do the following:

Intellectual Development Focus: Pray that the Holy Spirit will increase your intellectual power. Ask Him to give you the ability to comprehend His Word as you read and attend teaching sessions of the church. Also ask Him to show you how to be committed to education through the schools of the church and other areas of study.

Physical Development Focus: Pray that the Spirit will help you eat right on a daily basis by following this diet. Ask Him to help you become a physical fitness role model to others. Ask God to show you how to preserve your body for the Holy Spirit to live. Also ask Him to show you how to be committed to physical development and not renege.

Spiritual Development Focus: Ask God to help you grow closer to Him and to show you how to build a good relationship with Him. Ask Him to give you the strength to keep Him first in your life. Also ask Him to show you how to be committed to worship and prayer-related activities.

Social Development Focus: Ask Christ to show you how to build good relationships. Ask Him to help you love people more sincerely. Ask God to put great people in your life who can help you reach your goals. If you are single and hope to get married, don't be afraid to ask the Holy Spirit to send you the person He wants you to spend the rest of your life with. Be sure to ask the Holy Spirit to increase your love for community. The good thing about this kind of prayer is you can repeat it anytime if you should fall off the wagon with the same purpose.

One thing to remember is this: if you can eat cabbage soup, fruit, vegetables, and salads with very little meat and no bread for seven days, you have just discovered a new eating plan you were successful at doing. Therefore, it becomes much easier for you to develop a good plan for daily food balance afterward.

The prayer diet fast was perfect for my wife and me. We stuck it out for seven days, and together we lost eighteen pounds and about six inches from our waists. I was even able to wear my polo shirts on the inside again. From this point, we began looking for a plan to maintain our success. The fact is most people can go on a diet and lose weight, but that's not enough unless you have a plan to help keep the weight from reappearing.

I was praying and asking God to show us what to do after we completed the fast. We needed a plan for eating for the first seven days after the initial diet was complete. We needed a workable plan we could teach to the church members so they wouldn't revert back to the same old eating habits, which had already damaged many. We also needed a plan that would produce excitement as we waited on different times of the week to eat certain foods.

In answer to our prayer, Christ gave us a plan called organized eating. This is a plan to make people feel good about their eating decisions at the end of the day. For example, Friday will be steak and potato day. Everyone looks forward to Friday because we only get this kind of meat once or twice a week. The reason for this is so we don't get accustomed to eating like this every day. Eating too much meat may have already gotten some people in bad shape. Every day cannot be a celebration of the same kind of food. Maybe once a week we will celebrate with stir-fry as our main entrée or some other great-tasting healthy meal. Whatever the meals are for the week, they must be eaten in moderation—first, so we can maintain good health, and second, so we don't stretch our stomach again. We advised them to stay away from sweets as much as possible unless they were ready to go back to the cabbage soup for another seven days. This plan is only to get them started, and then they can create their own plan as long as they keep the same idea in their meal preparation.

Organized Eating Plan

Monday

Breakfast: Eat as much fruit as you want. Cut it up and arrange it on your plate in an appealing way that makes you want to eat it. If you need a snack later, eat some more fruit. It just gets you ready for lunch.

Lunch: All the vegetables you can eat, cooked or raw, and a bowl of soup and fruit of your choice. If you need a snack later, eat some more vegetables! It just makes you ready for dinner.

Dinner: Stir-fry over a bed of brown rice. Eat no meat other than the chicken strips used in the stir-fry. This is amazingly good and filling.

Tuesday

Breakfast: Frosted Mini-Wheats with a cut-up banana to add extra flavor. This will actually hold you until lunch.

Lunch: Tuna salad, along with a few crackers and fruit of your choice.

Dinner: Oven-baked chicken with no skin, along with some black-eyed peas or pinto beans.

Wednesday

Breakfast: Oatmeal mixed with raisins, walnuts, and brown sugar.

Lunch: Raw vegetables with veggie dip and fruit of your choice

Dinner: Potato soup with a healthy salad mixed with cucumbers and beets

Thursday

Breakfast: Two hard-boiled eggs and whole-wheat toast with butter and jelly.

Lunch: Peanut butter sandwich with wheat bread and fruit of your choice.

Dinner: Baked fish with brown pasta and a tossed salad.

Friday

Breakfast: Your choice of cereal.

Lunch: Sub sandwich of your choice.

Dinner: Steak with stewed tomatoes, along with a salad or roasted asparagus.

Saturday

Breakfast: One or two eggs and two slices of bacon or turkey sausage, served with toast.

Lunch: Vegetables and fruit, along with cottage cheese and fruit of your choice.

Dinner: Soup and salad.

Sunday

Breakfast: Cereal or oatmeal.

Lunch: Fruit with a cup of yogurt.

Dinner: Baked chicken and broccoli or mixed vegetables or turnip greens.

This plan has worked tremendously for us. The challenge is to stick with it and discover its amazing rewards. You will feel good and sleep good, and your body will look good, which results in you doing well. I really hope I shared something in this chapter that will motivate every reader to act on some of those healthy principles. I pray someone will find new life through the ideas I've shared. It's time for people in general to start taking their health more seriously than ever before. If you act on some of the things I've shared, your life will be changed forever, and you will feel better and look better than ever before. If you don't like this plan, please feel free to write one you can stick with. Don't let the plan become boring; mix it up as often as you can to keep it exciting. God will help you as you pray for different eating ideas. The Scripture encourages us to make plans.

We should make plans—counting on God to direct us. (Prov. 16:9 TLB)

The vision God gave me is really affecting change in the physical development area of our membership. Everyone has become health conscious and is looking for ways to improve their lives through diet and exercise. As I wrote this chapter, I sensed the hand of God upon me, giving me a sense of enthusiasm to motivate the people as He produced the ideas in my mind. Since the launch of the pray fast diet program, at least six people have tried it, and they all have lost ten to twenty pounds each and are now developing good eating habits to maintain their health. These people are pushing the idea throughout the church, declaring the hand of God as being upon our ministries. If you are not sure about whether you are healthy enough to participate in any parts of the outlined physical development programs, please check with your doctor before getting started.

Think healthy; whatever your daily eating plan is, it needs to be written and made plain because it will be the vision for your daily diet.

Write the vision, and make it plain ... (Hab. 2:2 GNB)

Chapter 6

Spiritual Development

hapter 6 brings focus to another area of development that sets Jesus apart from others called spiritual development. Spiritual development deals with the relationship Jesus has with His Father, which He practiced on a daily basis. Growing into a relationship with Christ is the best thing that could happen to a human being because it will fulfill the person's very purpose. God made us to love and to have a relationship with Him. Out of all His creations, He gave us alone the capacity to love Him back. The development of this relationship also sets us apart from the rest of His creations, making us special to Him. Jesus didn't just become spiritual; He grew to be spiritual, according to our vision Scripture.

Jesus grew in wisdom and stature, and in favor with God and men. (Luke 2:52 NIV)

"Growing in favor with God" is about Jesus being loved and blessed by His Father while He pleased Him with His life. His desire was to be a model to humankind by leading them to love God and to worship Him with their whole hearts and to put nothing before Him. He made it clear in Scripture that loving God is the greatest thing a person could do.

> Jesus replied: "Love the Lord your God with all your heart and with all your soul and with all your mind." This is the first and greatest commandment. (Matt. 22:37–38 NIV)

The development of this vertical relationship is to put God above everything else in your life. It is to surrender all unto Him. This makes the relationship special. Developing this kind of relationship with God will fulfill the first four of the Ten Commandments God gave His people. These four commandments deal with our relationship with Him only.

> Thou shalt have no other gods before me. Thou shalt not make unto thee any graven image, or any likeness of any thing that is in heaven above, or that is in the earth beneath, or that is in the water under the earth: … Thou shalt not take the name of the Lord thy God in vain; for the Lord will not hold him guiltless that taketh his name in vain. Remember the sabbath day, to keep it holy. (Ex. 20:3–4, 7–8 KJV)

Obedience to these four commandments builds a love relationship between us and God, and they are the most important of the commandments because they help us grow spiritually, resulting in us walking in God's divine favor and experiencing Him as Jesus did. I believe this kind of growth starts with feeding the spiritual part of us certain things. Just as our bodies need a consistent supply of food and exercise to be strong and healthy, the spiritual part of us must likewise be nurtured with the right kind of food.

I believe there are certain habits we must have and practice daily to grow in favor with God that will help us reach spiritual maturity. The rest of this chapter will focus on a few of the habits necessary to grow spiritually in the eyes of God.

Habit Number One: Studying the Word of God

The first habit to building a strong spiritual life with God is the habit of studying His Word. Studying the Word of God should be as important to us as eating. In fact, the Word of God is our spiritual food, and we must partake of it daily for continual growth. The need for the Word of God to be active in our lives is seen several times in Scripture. The writer of Hebrews makes it plain that we need the word to grow up as Christians.

> For every one that useth milk is unskilful in the word of righteousness: for he is a babe. But strong meat belongeth to them that are of full age, even those who by reason of use have their senses exercised to discern both good and evil. (Heb. 5:13–14 KJV)

> Therefore let us leave the elementary teachings about Christ and go on to maturity, not laying again the foundation of repentance from acts that lead to death, and of faith in God. (Heb. 6:1 NIV)

The use of these two verses in our lives will help us mature and do the things necessary to promote spiritual growth.

The Bible is the infallible Word of God written by men under the inspiration of the Holy Spirit. As such, any person who wants to reach spiritual maturity must develop the fundamental practice of spending time studying God's Word. It is only by carefully examining the Word of God that we discover His true nature and have the assurance that our walk is in alignment with His direction for our lives.

The Holy Bible is one book made up of sixty-six smaller books. There are thirty-nine Old Testament books and twenty-seven New Testament books. The Bible recounts the history of God's covenant with His people. The Old Testament relates the story of the creation of the world, the fall of man, the establishment of the Jews as God's chosen people, and their struggle to maintain their relationship with God. In the Old Testament, we find several amazing faith-building stories, such as how Moses led the Jews out of Egypt, how God rescued Daniel from the lion's den, how Elijah called fire down from heaven to destroy the prophets of Baal, and how He delivered the Hebrew boys from the burning furnace. The Scripture says,

For whatsoever things were written aforetime were written for our learning, that we through patience and comfort of the Scriptures might have hope. (Rom. 15:4 KJV)

The New Testament, as the name indicates, is the new covenant God has with His people. What could not be accomplished through the Law is now possible through God's Son, Jesus. The New Testament makes it known that through Jesus Christ, all people can have a relationship with God, not just a chosen few. Beginning with the birth of Jesus, the New Testament is filled with hope and promises of an eternal union with God and Jesus as our Savior.

God gave us the Bible to teach us the truth so we can know the truth according to His Word. While there is no best way to study the Word, there are several key practices that allow our study to be more effective. Setting aside quiet time will help us tune out distractions so we can focus on what we are reading. Using a high-quality study Bible with detailed explanations of Scriptures, cross-referencing data, maps, a dictionary, and a concordance are tools that will help us gain a better understanding of the biblical world and the context of the events during which the Bible was written. As we read with an open heart, God will begin to reveal the meaning and application of the Word to us. The Word is the mind of God; therefore, it must be handled with care. The Scripture says we must study it to keep from being made ashamed as we communicate it to others.

> Study to shew thyself approved unto God, a workman that needeth not to be ashamed, rightly dividing the word of truth. (2 Tim. 2:15 KJV)

Habit Number Two: Memorizing the Word

One of the most powerful habits a person can develop is to memorize Scripture. As you put the Word in your mind, it will come to you when you need it most. Committing the Word of God to memory helps us make wise decisions, gives us peace in times of stress, and assists us in sharing the gospel with others. When we memorize Scriptures, we have more opportunities to solve problems or to give a word of encouragement. There is nothing greater than being able to help someone through God's Word. When we are facing the greatest temptations of our lives, the Word of God will help us come through the trial. It will help us say no to sin, no matter how tempting it may be. The wise man Solomon encourages us to keep the Word in our hearts.

> Guard my words as your most precious possession. Write them down, and also keep them deep within your heart. (Prov. 7:2–3 TLB)

The Word of God is the greatest gift we will ever have in our lives and in our homes. It will lead us, guide us, and protect us if we keep it in our hearts. David also makes reference to keeping the Word in our hearts.

I have hidden your Word in my heart that I might not sin against you. (Ps. 119:11 NIV)

I love the idea of hiding the Word in our hearts. We hide the Word in our hearts when we study and apply it through memorization. When we hide the Word in our hearts, it becomes part of our decision-making process, as the Word instructs us:

For which of you, intending to build a tower, sitteth not down first, and counteth the cost, whether he have sufficient to finish it? (Luke 14:28 NIV)

Not only do we need the Word in us for decision making, but we need it more so because of its nature in that it never dies and it never stops performing.

For the word of God is living and active. Sharper than any double-edged sword, it penetrates even to dividing soul and spirit, joints and marrow; it judges the thoughts and attitudes of the heart. (Heb. 4:12 NIV)

Once the Word is in your heart, it becomes alive and active in your decisions. It is so powerful that it cuts and penetrates; it judges your thoughts and the attitudes of your heart. The Word of God will let you know when you are wrong and when your motives are good or bad. This is why we need to apply the Word to memorization. God's Word is there to protect us in our day-to-day walk with Him. When we memorize the Word, it provides light over our path as we walk according to Scripture.

Thy word is a lamp unto my feet, and a light unto my path.
(Ps. 119:105 NIV)

To follow the Word is to follow Christ, who will be with you in darkness providing light as you develop into spiritual maturity. Jesus makes it even clearer in this verse:

I am the light of the world. Whoever follows me will never walk in darkness, but will have the light of life. (John 8:12 NIV)

Habit Number Three: Meditating On The Word

Meditation is focused thinking. It is to ponder on what God is saying to you in His Word. It is being in deep thought on how you can apply the Word to your personal life. A good example of a meditative instruction Scripture is this verse:

Finally, brothers, whatever is true, whatever is noble, whatever is right, whatever is pure, whatever is lovely, whatever is admirable—if anything is excellent or praiseworthy—think about such things. (Phil. 4:8 NIV)

Meditating on the Word of God helps us find the best in others. It removes negative thoughts from our minds as we discover things lovely and admirable in people. When we find things in people that are praiseworthy, we begin thanking God for those people being in our lives. You can't think about the excellence of people and hate on them at the same time. Any time you have negative thoughts about people, just start looking for their good side and you will find they are great people to have in your life. The Bible declares in other passages of Scripture the benefits of meditation in the Word:

Blessed is the man who does not walk in the counsel of the wicked or stand in the way of sinners or sit in the seat of mockers. But his delight is in the law of the Lord, and on his law he meditates day and night. He is like a tree planted by streams of water, which yields its fruit in season and whose leaf does not wither. Whatever he does prospers. (Ps. 1:1–3 NIV)

According to these verses, we have the choice to focus on the ways of sin or to meditate on the promises of God. The Word tells us if we choose God and focus on what He has to say to us, we will be like trees planted by the riverbank. Proper nourishment will allow us to produce fruit in our season, and because of our commitment, whatever we do will prosper.

Focused thinking on the Word of God will place us in a position to receive God's promises. Joshua says,

Do not let this Book of the Law depart from your mouth; meditate on it day and night, so that you may be careful to do everything written in it. Then you will be prosperous and successful. (Josh. 1:8 NIV)

Joshua makes it plain that if we want to be blessed by God, prosperous and successful, we must keep the Word of God in our mouths and think about it every day so we can do what the Word says. Meditation assists us in our efforts to be obedient to the Word; once we learn to obey the Word, we will experience the blessings it brings. There are so many people in the world who are praying for a blessing and hoping to find favor with God. Our greatest blessings come through obeying the Word. Joshua says we should meditate on the Word day and night so we can obey what it says, resulting in us being prosperous and successful. God wants to bless us, but there are conditions accompanying His promises.

The more time we spend meditating on the Word, the more transformed our thinking becomes, which leads to a transformed lifestyle. What we feed our minds is what we will soon become. This is the reason why Paul encouraged us to not follow the world's ideas for living.

> Do not conform any longer to the pattern of this world, but
> be transformed by the renewing of your mind. Then you will
> be able to test and approve what God's will is—his good,
> pleasing and perfect will. (Rom. 12:2 NIV)

In other words, don't let the world squeeze you into its mold. Don't let the world shape your thinking or entice you with its habits, entertainments, and recreations. He is calling us to be transformed through the renewing of our minds. We renew our minds through meditating on the Word, thinking about the good things in life, staying positive in the midst of negative circumstances, and being optimistic about God at all times. Thinking like this will help us discover God's good and perfect will for our lives.

Habit Number Four: Prayer

Prayer is a personal communication between God and His people. It is a key element for spiritual maturity. Praying to God proves we have faith in Him. Praying and believing God will answer is an act of faith. God speaks to us through His Word, and we talk to Him through prayer. Through our prayers, we develop a relationship with God. Once our relationship is established, we will begin to view Him as our Creator, our Helper, our Healer, and the source of our strength. It is by having this kind of relationship with Christ that we can speak as the apostle Paul spoke with great confidence.

I can do everything through him who gives me strength. (Phil. 4:13 NIV)

Though there are many types of prayers, there is no right or wrong way to pray. Jesus taught his disciples to pray using the following words:

This, then, is how you should pray: "Our Father in heaven, hallowed be your name, your kingdom come, your will be done on earth as it is in heaven. Give us today our daily bread. Forgive us our debts, as we also have forgiven our debtors. And lead us not into temptation, but deliver us from the evil one. (Matt. 6:9–13 NIV)

This is a perfect example for anyone learning to pray because it contains all the elements necessary for a proper prayer. First and foremost, God is given honor and praise when we acknowledge Him as "our Father in heaven," whose name is hallowed, meaning to be blessed, sanctified, and holy. We welcome His purpose when we ask Him to let His kingdom come and His will be done on earth or in us as it is in heaven. It proves who we trust for provision when we ask Him to give us our daily bread and when we recognize it is Him alone who sustains us and provides for our needs. We make Him happy when we ask Him to help us with the tough things we can't handle by forgiving our sins as we forgive those who sin against us so we can maintain good relationships with others. We make Him happy when we admit it is He alone who can lead us around temptation and protect us from the evil one. Finally, we close the prayer by acknowledging the extent of His attributes in being the kingdom, the power, and the glory forever, amen.

This simple prayer beautifully outlines the structure used for other types of prayers, regardless of specifics. Prayers can be anything from a simple request for guidance to sophisticated devotions of worship and adoration. Now I want to explore a few of the different prayers people pray.

Prayer of Confession

Prayers of confession bring us back into fellowship with God when we have sinned, according to the Word,

> If we confess our sins, he is faithful and just and will forgive us our sins and purify us from all unrighteousness. (1 John 1:9 NIV)

We know God loves us and wants nothing but the best for us. When we pray and ask for forgiveness for any sins we have committed and walk away from them by giving them up, it opens the door for His mercy to work in our lives to restore our relationship with Him.

> He who conceals his sins does not prosper, but whoever confesses and renounces them finds mercy. (Prov. 28:13 NIV)

Prayer of Thanksgiving

The more we grow spiritually, the more we will be mindful to thank God for all the wonderful things He has done for us, just as the psalmist instructs us:

Give thanks to the Lord, for he is good; his love endures forever. (Ps. 107:1 NIV)

Prayers of thanksgiving are essential because they solidify God as our provider. It is always appropriate to spend time reflecting on the goodness of the Lord. During this time, you will uncover more and more things to be thankful for, such as peace of mind, a good job, and a healthy and loving family. Once we are in the habit of giving thanks, we will even find ourselves thanking God for the little things, such as a good parking spot or a refreshing glass of cold water on a hot summer day. Prayers of thanksgiving can also be anticipatory, looking forward. Those prayers release your faith and thanks to God in advance for all the things He will do in the future.

Prayer of Healing

Our healing is no greater than our faith. If we believe God can heal, we must live our lives accordingly. There are several stories in Scripture given to increase our faith when it comes to healing. One story is the woman who had an issue of blood. Jesus healed her because of her faith.

Daughter, your faith has healed you. Go in peace. (Luke 8:48 NIV)

The Bible says she spent all her money on doctors trying to find a cure, but nothing worked. Even though she was weak from the illness, she refused to be defeated. Relying on faith, she made her way to see Jesus even though there was already a large crowd around Him. She pushed her way through the crowd to get to Him. The Bible tells us when she touched Him, she was immediately healed. Jesus said to her, "Daughter, your faith has healed you. Go in peace." This story perfectly illustrates how prayer and faith work together. Another story is found in Matthew 8. Jesus healed the Roman Army captain's servant. The servant was sick in bed and racked with pain. The healing came because of the captain's faith.

> Then the officer said, "Sir, I am not worthy to have you in
> my home; [and it isn't necessary for you to come]. If you will
> only stand here and say, 'Be healed,' my servant will get well!"
> (Matt. 8:8 TLB)

The centurion felt he was not worthy to have Jesus in his home. He believed Jesus could heal his servant without even coming to his home. His level of faith was so strong he believed Jesus could heal his servant from where He was just by speaking the Word.

> I know, because I am under the authority of my superior officers
> and I have authority over my soldiers, and I say to one, "Go,"
> and he goes, and to another, "Come," and he comes, and to my
> slave boy, "Do this or that," and he does it. And I know you have
> authority to tell his sickness to go—and it will go! (Matt. 8:9 TLB)

The centurion compared his own authority with the authority of Jesus. As an army captain, his men responded and obeyed without questioning him whenever he told them what to do. He felt if he a mere man could get this kind of response from people, Jesus, having more authority than he did, could tell the sickness to go and it would go! Because of that, Jesus said,

> Jesus stood there amazed! Turning to the crowd he said, "I
> haven't seen faith like this in all the land of Israel!" (Matt.
> 8:10 TLB)

Then Jesus said to the centurion, "Go! It will be done just as you believed it would." And his servant was healed at that very hour." (Matt. 8:13 NIV)

As people of God, we must understand healing always follows faith in God. Prayer gets us to our knees, but faith is what unlocks the doors. The writers of Hebrews and James made this clear when they wrote about faith.

And without faith it is impossible to please God, because anyone who comes to him must believe that he exists and that he rewards those who earnestly seek him. (Heb. 11:6 NIV)

But when he asks, he must believe and not doubt, because he who doubts is like a wave of the sea, blown and tossed by the wind. That man should not think he will receive anything from the Lord; he is a double-minded man, unstable in all he does. (James 1:6–8 NIV)

These two verses prove that, without faith, there is no need to ask God for anything. There is more to prayer than just praying; it's about believing God will answer your prayers and walking according to your belief in His Word; that's faith!

Habit Number Five: Private and Public Worship

Worship is defined as an act of spiritual devotion to God. Corporate worship is a group of believers who come together to express their love to God in a public and structured setting. Everything we do, including our songs, dances, sermons, testimonies, and services, represents how much we love the Lord.

When we praise the Lord with the integrity of our hearts, we can actually feel His presence within us, and all those with open hearts will be touched by His power. I believe our praise is what opens the door and invites the Lord to dwell among us. Private worship, as opposed to corporate public worship, is a special form of godly adoration experienced when we are alone. This most often happens during quiet and intimate times with Him. When we are praying or studying the Word of God, we often sense the presence of the Lord in the room and hear His voice speaking directly to us.

Although each individual experience is different, during private worship, it is common to become overwhelmed with a deep feeling of love and appreciation for the Lord. As we pray and reflect on His power, mercy, and faithfulness, our hearts become filled with gratitude and humility. This feeling is often such an intense spiritual experience that it compels many to renounce their sins and to reaffirm their commitment and dedication to the Lord. Consistent private worship keeps us close to God by keeping our hearts and minds open to His will.

Taken together, public and private worship opens the door for the Lord's power, grace, and favor to work in our lives. When we show we are devoted to the Lord through our praise and worship, God gives us power to walk in victory over the temptations and negative situations we face in our everyday lives. Worship empowers us to defeat the Devil's strategy, as seen with Jesus.

Jesus said to him, "Away from me, Satan! For it is written: 'Worship the Lord your God, and serve him only.'" (Matt. 4:10 NIV)

Worship keeps our focus on God. When we are going through our most trying moments with people and the temptations the world offers, worshipping God is what brings us through and gives us the victory. Sometimes, without being consciously aware of it, our praise and worship lead us to fulfill the Great Commission. As people watch us worship, they learn how to worship God and make decisions for Christ following the worship experience. The psalmist verified this when he said these words:

> He put a new song in my mouth, a hymn of praise to our
> God. Many will see and fear and put their trust in the Lord.
> (Ps. 40:3 NIV)

If our worship is real, people will see Christ in us, establish respect for Him, and put their trust in Him because of what they see in us. We must be mindful at all times and in every worship service that there will always be people watching us as we worship. Therefore, it would behoove us to properly prepare ourselves for worship by learning the songs, lifting our hands and voices in praise, and praying during the worship so we can be as real as possible for Christ and for those who are watching and learning from us.

Habit Number Six: The Habit of Giving

The final habit in developing our spiritual lives is the habit of giving. Worship and giving go together. There are more Scriptures in the Bible about giving than any other topic, including salvation. Obviously, giving is very important to God and is part of the foundation of the Christian life. Giving makes us like God, who gave His only Son as an act of love toward us.

> For God so loved the world that he gave his one and only Son,
> that whoever believes in him shall not perish but have eternal
> life. (John 3:16 NIV)

No gift can be given that is greater than the gift God gave. He loved us so much that He gave His only Son for us. Love is an action on behalf of others, and giving is a sure way to test your love to see if it is real. The Corinthians were encouraged to grow in their giving because giving is the greatest expression of love. Paul encouraged them with these words:

But since you excel in everything—in faith, in speech, in knowledge, in complete earnestness and in the love we have kindled in you—see that you also excel in this grace of giving. (2 Cor. 8:7 NIV)

In this verse, giving is equated with other essential Christian principles, such as faith, speech, knowledge, earnestness, and love. This means giving is an integral part of a successful Christian life. The Bible notes two principal forms of giving God expects every believer to practice, called tithes and offerings. Allow me to expound a little on these two serious expectations.

First I will emphasize tithes. Tithing is giving a tenth of our income back to the Lord. Scripture stresses what part of our income we should give to the Lord and how it will benefit us if we are obedient.

Honor the Lord by giving him the first part of all your income, and he will fill your barns with wheat and barley and overflow your wine vats with the finest wines. (Prov. 3:9 TLB)

The first part of our income represents the best part and the untouched part. This kind of giving is putting God above everything else, making Him your number-one priority. God deserves more than what's left. He deserves being honored from the top of the pile, not the bottom. The first part is defined as the first 10 percent of our income, which should be set apart for God's purpose, according to the Scripture,

"Bring the whole tithe into the storehouse, that there may be food in my house. Test me in this," says the Lord Almighty, "and see if I will not throw open the floodgates of heaven and pour out so much blessing that you will not have room enough for it." (Mal. 3:10 NIV)

During Malachi's day, the reason for tithing was to ensure food was in the Lord's house. The people were holding back their tithes, knowing the Levites depended on it for their living. The people ignored their responsibility in caring for the temple and worship, which caused the Levites to have to work outside of the temple to earn their living. Tithing was God's plan for their livelihood. God said,

I give to the Levites all the tithes in Israel as their inheritance in return for the work they do while serving at the Tent of Meeting. (Num. 18:21 NIV)

The tithes ensured the temple had ample food and provision for the people God had planned to care for. When the serving ministers have to work outside of their calling, the house of God will be neglected. I tried to pastor and work outside the church for three years, and it just did not work. I discovered you can't get very much done for the church. As a matter of fact, God kept things hidden from me because I didn't have time to do it. If He had shown me, being a pastor, I would have tried to make it happen because of the calling to lead, but it would have only brought about more aggravations in my life.

Being a father, husband, employee, and leader of the church is way too much for one man. Something will definitely be neglected, and most of the time it's going to be your wife and children and the church. I speak out of experience. The church work alone is more than one man can handle, and it would benefit church members to pay tithes so they can allow the pastor to retire if he works outside of the church. This way God can reveal the work that's being kept from him so the church can grow to spiritual maturity.

Before people decide not to pay tithes, they really need to take a serious look at what the Scripture has to say about the purpose for tithing. The purpose is made undeniably clear in this verse:

The purpose of tithing is to teach you always to put God first in your lives. (Deut. 14:23 TLB)

Tithing teaches us to always make God first in all we have. It teaches us to seek God first in our finances. It proves we really love God and care about what His Word says to us. Tithing reminds us from whom our income comes. The Scripture makes it plain that it's not out of our own gifts, strength, or knowledge that we have our jobs to care for our families, but rather they come from the Lord.

But remember the Lord your God, for it is he who gives you the ability to produce wealth. (Deut. 8:18 NIV)

If we acknowledge that it is the Lord who has given us the ability to get wealth, then we must also acknowledge that part of the wealth belongs to Him. This shows we have the character of God and are willing to obey Him in everything.

Second I will emphasize offerings. The offering is what we give over and above the tithe. Unlike tithes, offerings are not specifically defined in Scriptures as to how much it should be. It can be of any amount we choose, as long as it is given with the right attitude, as instructed in the Scriptures.

> Each man should give what he has decided in his heart to give, not reluctantly or under compulsion, for God loves a cheerful giver. And God is able to make all grace abound to you, so that in all things at all times, having all that you need, you will abound in every good work. (2 Cor. 9:7–8 NIV)

Whatever the offering is, one must know what one wants to give and not feel forced to give it but do so out of pure love and happiness. If we can't give it this way, it is not pleasing to God. When we give the offering in the proper manner, God will see that we abound in Him, having everything we need and able to be a blessing to others. Since an offering is a voluntary gift, it shows our appreciation to God. What we give back to the Lord in appreciation for what He has done for us is truly a reflection of how we feel about Him. Giving proves what we love most in life. It tracks our mind and hearts to what is important to us.

> For where your treasure is, there your heart will be also.
> (Matt. 6:21 NIV)

Jesus says to us that our minds and concerns will be on whatever is most important to us. If our money is the most important thing in our lives, our minds will be on money instead of God. When money is the most important thing in our lives, it will affect our relationship with God and people. You can't love both God and money, for one will truly be hated. The Scripture says,

No one can serve two masters. Either he will hate the one and love the other, or he will be devoted to the one and despise the other. You cannot serve both God and Money. (Matt. 6:24 NIV)

I have met people throughout my life who were truly in love with money. Money was all they ever talked about. Everything in their lives was built around it. I have met some who work seven days a week, jeopardizing the relationship of their families and churches, to make more money. Many are so busy making money that they don't take the proper time to spend it. They never shop because they possess a miser mentality. They are so cheap that they have missed out on what real life is about. They think life is all about what they own. Jesus made it clear in Scripture that this is not the way of life when He said,

Watch out! Be on your guard against all kinds of greed; a man's life does not consist in the abundance of his possessions. (Luke 12:15 NIV)

Life is about more than what we own; real life is about a real relationship with Christ and people. It's a life that is shared with others through our resources. Following Jesus' challenge about greed is a story about a man who had so many goods that he didn't have room to store them; rather than sharing them with other people who were less fortunate, he said to himself that he would build bigger barns to store them. Afterward he would say to himself he had plenty and would encourage himself to take it easy; to eat, drink, and be merry. God challenged him with these words:

But God said to him, "You fool! This very night your life will be demanded from you. Then who will get what you have prepared for yourself?" (Luke 12:20 NIV)

I believe spiritual maturity becomes evident in our lives when we use our resources to help make the world better by helping people who can't help themselves and to continue the work of Christ. When we recognize our giving supports the work of the Christ, we will become committed to pleasing God with it. A spiritually mature person recognizes the importance of giving and does not neglect this habit.

Spiritual Development Programs

Our spiritual programs consist mostly of the things we do to advance worship. Some of the current programs are choir singing, praise team singing, dance ministry, worship leaders' ministry, and prayer ministry. Our hope with all of them is to lead people to a place with God they have not been since the last corporate worship service and to have an experience with Him they haven't had since the last time.

To keep us on point with our worship dream, there are three areas we focus on that cover all we do: "Impact worship, impact worship promise, and impact prayer." They help us with balance as we develop our lives spiritually.

Impact Worship/Singing

Our goal for singing is to get the congregation involved by singing songs to which they can relate. When they stand during the first two upbeat songs, they are encouraged to sing, clap their hands, bounce, jump, and dance; in other words, to enjoy God. We put the words of the songs on a big screen to make it easy for them to participate. When the music changes to a slower pace, we don't ask them to stand because we want them to make a connection with God and stand all because they feel inspired and convicted to do so.

We plan our worship weekly by sitting down with the key

worship leaders and assessing what was good and not so good each week. We create an order of service in advance to help us do a proper evaluation. We ask questions concerning the songs one at a time as they appear on the order of service, considering if they will accomplish our goals for the service. Then we focus on the creativity of the service, seeking ways to enhance the worship through things like media, dance, and flags that will help usher people into the presence of God. Each evaluation session takes about two hours, and we don't stop until we somewhat enter the place and feel the experience we want them to have on Sunday.

It is critical for the leaders of worship to experience God first before any other part of worship is developed. We have to know what the service will be like before Sunday morning. We have more successful worship services by doing this than we did before we started the planning and evaluation process. I believe God is well-pleased with us planning our worship. The Scripture tells us,

We should make plans—counting on God to direct us. (Prov. 16:9 TLB)

Impact Worship Promise

At every worship service, our goal is to impact the people's lives through worship. We don't know how people will come in, but we do know how they can leave. Our goal is to give them something to look forward to during their worship experience. Therefore, we promise them they will receive certain things from our worship that will have an impact on their lives. We use the four pillars/core values of the church to develop our promise to them.

Intellectual Pillar

Intellectually, we promise the members and the people we invite to our service that they will receive a message relevant for today that they can apply to their lives all week long—a message that will make them think, give them power, and connect them with God.

Physical Pillar

Physically, we promise the members and the people that we witness to about attending our church that they will experience a form of physical fitness in our worship services. This physical fitness will help them with any pain they might be experiencing as they stand and get involved, singing upbeat songs, clapping their hands, bouncing, jumping, and dancing as they praise God.

Spiritual Pillar

Spiritually, we promise the members and the people we witness to about attending our church that they will enter a place with God they have never been and have an experience with Him they have never had.

Social Pillar

Socially, we promise the members and the people we witness to about attending our church that they will meet people who have the same common needs they have, people who want to be their families—people who truly love people and want to share their lives with them.

These promises answer the questions many people ask after being invited to the worship at your church. "Why should I pass all the other churches to attend your church?" I believe if we can share with them what they can expect in a compelling, exciting way, it will increase our guest list tremendously.

Impact Prayer

Rather than having a few people praying on Sunday morning in a devotion service, we extend our prayer to cover many areas. The prayer team's focus is on praying during the week for specific needs. This team meets once a week for prayer at the church and to study prayer-related Scriptures. This team leads the people in fasting and praying for church growth and personal problems of the membership. They pray during the service that the worship will change lives and people will make a decision to accept Jesus Christ. They pray that God will perform miracles in the lives of the people. This team prays with each ministry that serves during the worship service. They also pray for me before I preach.

The prayer team leads a special prayer period every Wednesday for six months. During this time, they lead the congregation in a twelve-hour prayer vigil. The church is open at 8:00 a.m. and closes at 8:00 p.m. They encourage all worshippers to find at least a few minutes to stop by the church to talk to God. This is the greatest challenge a person can be given. Stopping by the church to pray for two to three minutes can be the hardest task to perform. Stopping by the church takes real sacrifice after you have put in a long and hard day at work. To leave a warm house in the winter season and go to the church to pray for two to three minutes takes real commitment. When they get to the church, they find soft, meditative music that leads them to a quiet time of worship and Scripture promises on the big screen that I taught them during the first six months of the year. I give them instructions on what to do after they have read and meditated on the Scripture and encourage them to continue practicing the word daily.

Chapter 7

Social Development

This chapter deals with the last area of development that Jesus' life was built upon. The Bible says Jesus grew in favor with men.

> And Jesus grew in wisdom and stature, and in *favor with* God and *men.* (Luke 2:52 NIV)

I believe growing in favor with men deals with social development, which relates to people and the environment in which they live. It deals with how people get along in the community, sharing their lives, valuing one another, and working together to serve a common goal. If people in our communities don't love and respect one another, it will be a place of chaos in which no one feels safe or comfortable. If our city is to be a city of values and standards, we must work together as a unified people to keep the environment healthy. Everyone must play their part in making it stable and balanced by keeping it free from negative societal interference. It is absolutely essential that every person and every family have a passion to see this development imparted into the lives of their children and grandchildren.

When it comes to social development, Jesus is our model. He was the best at connecting people. He understood people and knew how to meet their needs. Like Jesus, if we want people to follow us in our communities, we must offer them something greater than themselves, something that will make them proud of what they see. When Jesus worked miracles, He would leave people amazed and glorifying God, saying things like:

We never saw it on this fashion. (Mark 2:12 KJV)

People today want to see things in action rather than just hearing about them. People do not listen to churches or leaders in the community who don't have anything to offer. Today we must have a message, resources, and committed people to carry them out if the church is to gain the confidence of the people.

Jesus understood the value of community and how it affects the church of God. When people are transformed, our churches and communities are transformed as well. The more people we connect with in a God-fearing and positive environment, the better shape our neighborhoods, communities, cities, states, nation, and world will be. Social development is powerfully tied to community, and when people experience it, the entire city benefits. My hope is that after reading this chapter, people will be motivated to build social ties that are so strong that their communities will become (or remain) a safe place for them to live. Therefore, I will talk about social development with a focus on four different ways we can impact our community.

Impacting the Community through My Lifestyle

One of the greatest ways to connect with people is through my lifestyle. Lifestyle deals with more than what I say or do; it defines the integrity of my life. Some people talk about the Word while others are committed to doing what the Word says. Some people talk about the Christian life while others live the Christian life. When it comes to the church, some people are real, genuine, community- and kingdom-minded Christians, while others are just numbered among them. Some people are actually trying to make a difference in the world while others do not even think about their community or the world. When God saved us, He saved us to make a difference and gave us the tools necessary to help make society better. Our call as Christians should be seen in action on a daily basis, with us doing two things according to the Word of God.

Providing Seasoning to the Earth

Without seasoning, food just doesn't taste as good. Once it is applied, it stimulates the taste buds and causes us to enjoy it even more. Jesus makes it plain in the Scripture that we are the seasoning the world needs.

> You are the salt of the earth. But if the salt loses its saltiness, how can it be made salt again? It is no longer good for anything, except to be thrown out and trampled by men. (Matt. 5:13 NIV)

Jesus tells us in the verse above whose we are and why we were saved (which is to give hope to others through our personal lifestyles). Salt represents the authenticity of the character developed within us through the work of the Holy Spirit to influence a decaying world.

When people see us in the light or the dark, the representation of Christ must remain visible. Salt is a lifestyle that creates a thirst in others, making them desire Christ in their lives. Salt preserves and saves the world from evil by giving people a purpose and a cause that is greater than themselves. When our communities are properly seasoned, they give people hope and a purpose, making them want to impact the world.

Our task is to salt the community with the gospel of Jesus Christ through our lifestyles to prevent corruption. The bottom line is this: if Christians don't try to improve the world around them, they are of little value to the cause of Christ and lose their potential to influence the world and their communities. If we are too much like the world, we are ineffective. Christians should not blend in with everyone else. We must affect the world in the best way, just as seasoning brings out the best flavor in food. The second thing we must do in the world as Jesus' representatives is make light for the lost.

Making Light for the Lost

Jesus reveals who we are in the world and in our communities. He tells us exactly what we are supposed to be doing. When we connect with His purpose for our lives, we will be able to make the world better. We are the lights that shine for the world to see what the Christian life is like.

> You are the light of the world. A city on a hill cannot be hidden. Neither do people light a lamp and put it under a bowl. Instead they put it on its stand, and it gives light to everyone in the house. In the same way, let your light shine before men, that they may see your good deeds and praise your Father in heaven. (Matt. 5:14–16 NIV)

Our light is the outward testimony of the good works that validate our inner character. We make light through our witnessing and lifestyle. The good works we do in the world produce light that gives direction to people. This direction points them to the right path and connects them to God. The light we make will lead people out of their dark places of sinful activities. As long as people are walking in darkness, we cannot expect to see our world get any better. Wherever people are walking in darkness, there will always be communities in distress. We must lead them to the light where change can take place. Our light in the community represents the light of Jesus, and if people walk in it, they will be able to help finish what Jesus started long ago, saving souls and changing lives.

If we let our lights shine for Christ, we will glow like lamps, showing others what Christ is like and the kind of life He intended for us to live. We can never be caught hiding our lights because the purpose of having them is to lead others out of darkness and into the marvelous light of Jesus Christ. We hide our lights when we go along with the crowd and accept evil as if it is an acceptable way of life just because people are doing it. We hide our light by keeping our mouths closed when we should speak out. We can no longer act as if we are comfortable with the killings and drug trafficking in our communities. We must speak out against the things destroying our neighborhoods and resources. We hide our light by being conformed to the world's ideas for public pleasures. For this reason again, Paul warns us to not be overtaken by the pleasures of the world.

Do not conform any longer to the pattern of this world, but
be transformed by the renewing of your mind. Then you will
be able to test and approve what God's will is—his good,
pleasing and perfect will. (Rom. 12:2 NIV)

Conforming to the world will surely dim our lights in a way that causes others to not connect with Christ. The effects of conforming to the world's way of living are seen in the following verse:

> Be careful how you behave among your unsaved neighbors;
> for then, even if they are suspicious of you and talk against
> you, they will end up praising God for your good works when
> Christ returns. (1 Peter 2:12 TLB)

If we follow through with this information, we will be better equipped to impact our communities through our lifestyles. The second way we can impact our community is through building great relationships.

Impacting the Community through Relationships

According to Scripture, there are only two things that really matter to God; one is our love for Him, and the other is our love for each other, which is found in this these verses:

> Jesus replied: "'Love the Lord your God with all your heart
> and with all your soul and with all your mind.' This is the
> first and greatest commandment. And the second is like it:
> 'Love your neighbor as yourself.' All the Law and the Prophets
> hang on these two commandments." (Matt. 22:37–40 NIV)

Verse 37 deals with the first and greatest part: our love for God, which I talked about in chapter 6. The second part of what matters with God is in verse 39: our love for people. It is amazing how spiritual and social development work together to develop our love for God and people. It was for this reason God gave the Ten Commandments; the first four were for God, and the last six are for man. Any community can be healthy if those two factors are at work within it. In the following verses, we are encouraged to do six things to keep the community healthy:

> Honor your father and your mother, so that you may live long in the land the Lord your God is giving you. You shall not murder. You shall not commit adultery. You shall not steal. You shall not give false testimony against your neighbor. You shall not covet your neighbor's house. You shall not covet your neighbor's wife, or his manservant or maidservant, his ox or donkey, or anything that belongs to your neighbor. (Ex. 20:12–17 NIV)

Everything in these six commandments is there to help us live with each other and to protect us against evil. Think about all of them, and visualize the effects of these commandments, working together in our community and world. This is what you would see: Parents being honored by their children, children living long lives, and people dying only natural deaths because no one would be killed by anyone. There wouldn't be infidelity among the people or any form of sexual wrongdoing and disloyalty in relationships. People could leave their homes and not worry about break-ins or anything being taken from them. People would tell the truth and not lie about one another or give false reports, and no one would enviously desire another's possessions. This is what loving your neighbor is about, which many people need training in doing.

Social development deals with our love for one another, which is the only proof of our love for God. In fact, loving our neighbor is a reflection of our love for God. The Scripture teaches us that to love God is to love people and to love people is to love God.

If anyone says, "I love God," yet hates his brother, he is a liar.
For anyone who does not love his brother, whom he has seen,
cannot love God, whom he has not seen. (1 John 4:20 NIV)

How we treat one another will determine the outcome of our
environment. The more I do to help my neighbor, the more I show my
love for God. When I love my neighbors as myself, the relationship
among us will be life changing because I will do things for them as
though they were for me. I will serve them and not neglect them. I will
not cause any pain in their lives unless it is to help them. That's the kind
of love we are to have toward one another. Paul further details this love
with his love-evaluating passage, where he says,

Love is patient, love is kind. it does not envy, it does not boast,
it is not proud. It is not rude, it is not self-seeking, it is not easily
angered, it keeps no record of wrongs. Love does not delight in evil
but rejoices with the truth. It always protects, always trusts, always
hopes, always perseveres. Love never fails. (1 Cor. 13:4–8 NIV)

Love looks for ways to do right in relationships and how to improve
another person's life. Love builds people up and is not just concerned
about self. Love is putting the needs of others before your own. Again,
love is always thinking about how to make other people's lives better,
as the Word says,

Each of us should please his neighbor for his good, to build
him up. (Rom. 15:2 NIV)

This verse teaches us how important our neighbor should be to
us. We should consider the good of our neighbor and should look for

ways to build him up. So many times we only look at what is negative and overlook all the good in a person. As humans, we are quick to spot the bad in people yet expect our communities to be kind, loving, and compassionate. The best way to improve our community is to involve ourselves with others and compliment them on all the good they are doing and the difference they are making in the community. The fact is, we all need encouragement to keep up our good works. The wise man Solomon stated it well in the following verse:

You do yourself a favor when you are kind. (Prov. 11:17 GNB)

The truth is, when we help other people succeed, we succeed, and when they win, we win. With this in mind, we all must do more to show ourselves more loving toward the people God has put in our lives, whether they are saved or unsaved.

Social development shows us how to build great relationships with people. It teaches us how to approach people we may not know very well. In our communities, we must learn how to connect with people in a way that they will let us talk with them. Paul says that to build a relationship with people or to get them to listen to us, we must find common ground with them, as seen in the following Scriptures:

When I am with the Jews I seem as one of them so that
they will listen to the Gospel and I can win them to Christ.
When I am with Gentiles who follow Jewish customs and
ceremonies I don't argue, even though I don't agree, because I
want to help them. When with the heathen I agree with them
as much as I can, except of course that I must always do what
is right as a Christian. And so, by agreeing, I can win their
confidence and help them too. When I am with those whose

consciences bother them easily, I don't act as though I know it all and don't say they are foolish; the result is that they are willing to let me help them. Yes, whatever a person is like, I try to find common ground with him so that he will let me tell him about Christ and let Christ save him. I do this to get the Gospel to them and also for the blessing I myself receive when I see them come to Christ. (1 Cor. 9:20–23 TLB)

As we talk to people in the community, we must make a practice to listen so we can hear what is on their minds. We need to listen for a common-ground connection by discovering their hurts, needs, and interests. Once we find the connection, we can use it to develop a conversation that could lead them to Christ. We must build on the interest at hand if we want people to trust us. Once we show people, through the common-ground connection that we have been where they are and that we all have the same things in common, it makes them more receptive to what we have to say.

This does not mean you should compromise the gospel or your values while trying to make a connection. If we notice in the above verses, Paul points out some specifics: "I don't argue over customs, even though I don't believe in them." You cannot help people if you are turning them off by arguing with them about their beliefs. Paul said when he is with them, he seems like one of them, all because he wants to help them. He said that with the heathens, he agreed with them as much as he could. We have to look for whatever truth is being articulated and agree with it so we can get along and not fight. By agreeing with the truth, we can win their confidence. Remember, there is some truth in every conversation.

As Paul said, we can never, ever act like we know it all and expect people to let us talk to them about Christ or any other subject. I don't like this even among Christians today, and when this happens with me, it is not long before I depart. Paul says he agrees with them and does not act like he knows it all so he can get the gospel to them and for the blessing he will receive when he sees them come to Christ. Building relationships with people is one of the best things we can do because in the long run, we will need one another more than anything else. God made us for each other. He never intended for us to be alone but to be there for one another.

I remember the times when people really looked out for each other. If one had food, all had food. To fight one, you had to fight all. Those communities were built with strong ties. The question today is, how can we get back to this kind of community? Where do we start? We can start by retraining ourselves and then moving on to the community. Another way to impact the community is through sharing.

Impacting the Community through Sharing

Social development equips us to share our lives and stories with people. There are people who cross our paths every day: in grocery stores, schools, work, and other places where we are able to share Christ with. Jesus was the best at connecting with people, and the proof can be seen in His conversation with the woman at the well in a city called Sychar found in John chapter 4. Jesus showed her how to connect with God.

This story will show us how to impact the lives of people if we observe Jesus' approach. Jesus had just left Judea and was heading back to Galilee, but He needed to go through Samaria. I believe Jesus was rerouted through Samaria because there was a woman there who needed to be changed so she could influence many people in her city. There are two different conversations in this story that will help us understand the power of sharing or telling our stories in the community.

Jesus Shared with the Woman

When Jesus arrived, He found himself at Jacob's Well, weary and thirsty. At about the sixth hour, a woman came to the well to draw water and met Him. Jesus started a conversation with her. He said to her,

Will you give me a drink? (John 4:7 NIV)

The approach Jesus took with the woman was very simple. He didn't lunge at her in some rude fashion. He didn't ask her for anything hard to deliver, nor did He start off too intensely. He asked her for something she was familiar with—water. From there the conversation between Jesus and the woman began to build. The Samaritan woman said to Him,

You are a Jew and I am a Samaritan woman. How can you ask me for a drink? (For Jews do not associate with Samaritans.) (John 4:9 NIV)

What made Jesus so effective in His teaching is He always asked questions related to the answer He wanted to hear so He could help the person. No doubt Jesus knew the woman would connect His request for water with the relationship between the Jews and Gentiles and say, "How can you ask me for water when you know we don't get along?" Jesus didn't deny what she was saying. He knew it was true, but He didn't let prejudice get in the way of witnessing to this woman. He didn't argue about issues between them. He could have made an issue out of what she said, but He would not have accomplished His goal. He knew the Jews and Gentiles had racial issues with each other, but He bypassed this and went straight to the heart of the matter to make her think about to whom she was speaking. Jesus answered her, saying,

If you knew the gift of God and who it is that asks you for a drink, you would have asked him and he would have given you living water. (John 4:10 NIV)

When dealing with people we want to lead to Christ, we have to know what to say to not turn people away because we want to be argumentative. In the above verse, Jesus cut to the chase and said things to her to make her sense the gift of God in her presence. He said, "If you only knew the gift of God and who it is that ask you for a drink, you would have asked Him and He would have given you living water." Her response to Jesus shows she missed the message He was trying to give her.

"Sir," the woman said, "you have nothing to draw with and the well is deep. Where can you get this living water? Are you greater than our father Jacob, who gave us the well and drank from it himself, as did also his sons and his flocks and herds?" (John 4:11–12 NIV)

Like people today, the message of Christ was given to her, but her mind was not ready to receive it, so she kept talking about regular water. This tells me she did not understand what Jesus was saying. This is why we have to be experts in sharing the things of God or telling our stories about Christ—because people won't always comprehend what we are saying, and sometimes they might take our conversation off course with their answer. She didn't understand the true meaning of Jesus' words, and still thinking He was talking about natural water, she remarked that He didn't have anything to draw with and asked Him how she could get this living water.

This is a good lesson for us today; it helps us understand what to do in situations like these when we are taken off course. We have to know how to come back to the subject without losing people or treating them as if what they had to say didn't matter. The fact is, everything people say is of value to them, and we must respect what they have to tell us. Jesus made a smooth transition back to the subject.

> Everyone who drinks this water will be thirsty again, but whoever drinks the water I give him will never thirst. Indeed, the water I give him will become in him a spring of water welling up to eternal life. (John 4:13–14 NIV)

Jesus didn't get upset with the woman for missing the point. He didn't say, like many people would today, "You are missing what I am saying!" He just continued with the subject. He said when drinking the physical water, people would be thirsty again, but when they drank His water, they would never be thirsty. From there Jesus gave her a little more information. What He wanted her to know was physical water (things) will only satisfy the body, but the water He gives provides continual satisfaction. Jesus wanted the woman to know the person who drinks His living water will have a constant flow of water in him or her at all times. Based on her response, we see that she still didn't understand; the woman said to Him,

> Sir, give me this water so that I won't get thirsty and not have to keep coming here to draw water. (John 4:15 NIV)

Again, she reverted back to the regular water conversation. It's good that Jesus wasn't lost in His message for her. He knew at this point that He needed to change the subject to something she could understand and relate to. Jesus found another approach to His mission to save her. He told the woman,

"Go, call your husband and come back." "I have no husband," she replied. Jesus said to her, "You are right when you say you have no husband. The fact is, you have had five husbands, and the man you now have is not your husband. What you have just said is quite true." (John 4:16–18 NIV)

She may not have understood the living water conversation, but she truly understood her life. Jesus exposed her life right before her eyes, saying, "I know you don't have a husband. I also know how many you have had and what's going on right now in your life, and the man you have now isn't yours." This got her attention! I believe this was the beginning of change in her life. The evidence of change is seen in her response to Jesus.

"Sir," the woman said, "I can see that you are a prophet." (John 4:19 NIV)

Up to this point, she had made no reference to Jesus or God in this manner. It took a different kind of conversation to get her on the right path for an appropriate response; she saw Jesus as a prophet but not as one to seek for forgiveness. Rather, she changed the subject again and went to a worship conversation, which I believe sealed the deal on the part of Jesus' mission to get her saved. It appears the woman had a question she needed an answer to so she could make a decision. Read the following conversation:

"Our fathers worshiped on this mountain, but you Jews claim that the place where we must worship is in Jerusalem." Jesus declared, "Believe me, woman, a time is coming when you will worship the Father neither on this mountain nor in Jerusalem. You Samaritans worship what you do not know; we worship what we do know, for salvation is from the Jews. Yet a time is coming and has now come when the true worshipers will worship the Father in spirit and truth, for they are the kind of worshipers the Father seeks. God is spirit, and his worshipers must worship in spirit and in truth." The woman said, "I know that Messiah" (called Christ) "is coming. When he comes, he will explain everything to us." Then Jesus declared, "I who speak to you am he." (John 4:20–26 NIV)

Her concern was the location where the Jews said she and her fellow Samaritans were supposed to worship, which was in Jerusalem. He explained to her that the Jews worshipped in Jerusalem because salvation came to them first. Jesus made it clear that the time was coming when where you worshipped would not matter. He told her the time is now, and the true worshippers would worship God in spirit and in truth. God is spirit, and those who worship Him must worship Him in spirit and in truth. After hearing His explanation, she declared, "I know the Messiah (called Christ) is coming and when He comes, He will explain everything to us." To this Jesus replied, "I am the Christ."

Jesus didn't give up on her throughout this whole evangelistic approach. His commitment to save her shows us the importance of not giving up on people as we witness to them. If we are to make a difference in society, we must have a spirit of determination and not let other things sidetrack us from leading people to Christ. Seeing the outcome of Jesus' evangelistic work with the woman is enough to motivate us to improve our approach the next chance we get to witness.

The Woman Shares with the People

There is power in sharing the message of Christ. When we share, people are affected in a life-changing way, as seen with the people in the woman's town.

> Then, leaving her water jar, the woman went back to the town and said to the people, "Come, see a man who told me everything I ever did. Could this be the Christ?" They came out of the town and made their way toward him. (John 4:28–30 NIV)

The Scripture says she went back to town and told people what had happened and invited them in a compelling way to come see Jesus. She told her story, saying this man had told her everything about herself and everything she ever did. The people immediately responded by making their way toward Jesus. When they met Him, He ministered to them in such a way that they became believers. The impact of verse 41 tells us even more became believers because of His words, and they shared with the woman that they didn't need her story any longer because they "now knew for themselves."

> And because of his words many more became believers. They said to the woman, "We no longer believe just because of what you said; now we have heard for ourselves, and we know that this man really is the Savior of the world." (John 4:41–42 NIV)

It all started with Jesus sharing with the woman about living water, and then she told others about her encounter with Him. As a result of her testimony, people in her town believed in Christ. If we can get people to respond to us like the townspeople responded to the woman after hearing her testimonies about Jesus, many would be saved. It is for this very reason we are encouraged to develop our lives socially so we can impact our community with a message that will change lives forever.

Impacting the Community through Giving

Giving is a sure way to partake in community development. When we are socially involved through giving, we can help make a community difference. Until people are ready to invest into their communities, their surroundings will never get better. There are many ways we can give to improve society; we can give our time, talent, resources, and abilities to make things better for others.

One lesson I have learned about giving is when we give, we don't know who we are going to help by name, but we know someone will benefit. Oftentimes our giving helps people we don't know. The fact is, until we are ready to give without knowing who we will help, we are not ready to please God. When we built our church, many members we have today were not members, but they are sharing in the blessings of the building and ministry today. At the same time, the resources they are giving today will help people who are not yet members. For the next few pages, I want to engage your mind on the quality of the early church's giving.

Their Determination to Give

The quality of the early church's giving was phenomenal, which can be seen their zeal to share. The churches at Macedonia were so determined to help Paul make a difference in the lives of others that he used their determination to teach the church at Corinth. When you look at how determined they were to give, it will make you evaluate your own personal giving as it relates to the support of others.

And now, brothers, we want you to know about the grace that God has given the Macedonian churches. Out of the most severe trial, their overflowing joy and their extreme poverty welled up in rich generosity. (2 Cor. 8:1–2 NIV)

Because of their desire to give, the grace of God intervened. Though they had gone through a lot and really needed someone to help them in their most severe trials and extreme poverty, God's grace stepped in, took their joy and poverty, and gave birth to a generosity rich enough to help others. God's grace produced among them a generosity so rich that they gave in spite of their own hardships, enabling them to assist Paul in his financial drive. The grace in the text made all the difference. When I look at some of our communities and how rundown many of them are, I believe God will give us the grace necessary to have enough to give to make things better. Maybe we don't have much, but this same grace can be applied to us today. Grace can make joy and poverty work wonders together if our spirit and motives are right, like these churches.

The Extent of Their Giving

What made their giving so noteworthy was the extent of it. Many times I believe Christians are tested to see how far they will go to give to make a difference. Many people talk about giving but never produce anything. It seems like the ones who give the most are the ones who need the most help. When we see how much they are willing to give, our hearts can't help but be touched by their desire to give, as seen in these verses:

For I testify that they gave as much as they were able, and even beyond their ability. Entirely on their own, they urgently pleaded with us for the privilege of sharing in this service to the saints. (2 Cor. 8:3–4 NIV)

They gave as much as they were able and beyond their ability because they wanted to give. With this kind of mindset, there is nothing God will hold back from people who want to make a community difference. They loved God and people so much they were willing to go to the extreme to make something happen without looking for a returned favor. Paul said they urgently pleaded with him to help in this service. They didn't just plead but pleaded with a sense of urgency to act without delay.

The Perspective for Their Giving

They gave with the right perspective. Their perception for giving was on point. They didn't attempt to give in their own strength but rather through the power of God. Their giving was based upon their love and relationship with God. Paul spells it out in this verse:

And they did not do as we expected, but they *gave themselves first to the Lord* and then to us in keeping with God's will. (2 Cor. 8:5 NIV)

Giving themselves first to the Lord made all the difference. Once people learn to do this, giving will no longer be an issue with them.

The Attitude for Their Giving

This kind of giving is also about attitude. Paul expressed to the Corinthians the kind of attitude God is looking for when it comes to giving.

Each man should give what he has decided in his heart to give, not reluctantly or under compulsion, for God loves a *cheerful giver*. (2 Cor. 9:7 NIV)

Whatever it is one may give, it must be decided in his heart without anything hindering his desire. We cannot please God with our giving if we are reluctant for some reason or need it more than we are willing to give it. We should not feel pressured or forced to give because this kind of giving doesn't please God. Whatever we give to build up our communities, or to help people in any way, it must be given cheerfully, and when this happens, the next verse tells us what is possible.

And God is able to make all grace abound to you, so that in all things at all times, having all that you need, you will abound in every good work. (2 Cor. 9:8 NIV)

Paul is still talking about the same grace that caused the joy and extreme poverty of the Macedonian churches to store up rich generosity. After realizing the blessings available to them, people should be more motivated to trust God in their giving. In this way, we can bless our communities and be blessed ourselves at the same time. We can't beat God's giving because of the way He gives. If the desire is there, God makes the first move. Paul says,

And God, who supplies seed for the sower and bread to eat, will also supply you with all the seed you need and will make it grow and produce a rich harvest from your generosity. He will always make you rich enough to be generous at all times, so that many will thank God for your gifts which they receive from us. (2 Cor. 9:10–11 GNB)

Is there anything we can't do through giving? The above verses are full of promises for us to apply to our lives. God will supply the seed, increase your store of seed, enlarge your harvest, make you rich enough so you can give on every occasion, and produce thanksgiving to Him from others.

The Effect of Their Giving

When giving is from the heart, the effects are seen in many different ways. It makes others thank God for the blessings He gives to you. Paul puts it this way:

> This service that you perform is not only supplying the needs of God's people but is also overflowing in many expressions of thanks to God. Because of the service by which you have proved yourselves, men will praise God for the obedience that accompanies your confession of the gospel of Christ, and for your generosity in sharing with them and with everyone else. (2 Cor. 9:12–13 NIV)

Paul points out the effects of this kind of giving and how it touches in so many ways. He says it supplies the needs of God's people, along with producing many expressions of thanks to Him. This is what happens when we give with the right spirit; we touch lives for Christ, and He gets the glory. Paul says to them, "Because of the service you gave, you have proved yourselves." I believe they proved themselves to be doers of the Word and models of Jesus Christ, who gave His life for the church. He stamped it by saying men will praise God for the obedience accompanying their confession of the gospel of Christ that is seen through them sharing with others. Their action is in alignment with the Word, as seen also in this verse:

> Let your light shine before men, that they may see your good deeds and praise your Father in heaven. (Matt. 5:16 NIV)

Social Development Program

Hospitality

Hospitality is one of the key social development programs we use intentionally to connect with people during our worship service and any other services we host at our church. After the vision was made clear and written for the church, we enhanced the hospitality program we had by creating new ways to serve people other than just seating them. We created more ministry opportunities to serve the members and the guests at a level they had never been served before. As a result of this new idea, what we hear from guests more than anything is how special the members of the church make them feel.

I have witnessed on airplanes how the airline stewards stand at the door to greet people as they enter the plane. They all have bright smiles and say the things we want to hear. Their job is to make us feel we chose the right airline and that our flight will be safe. I have also noticed how Wal-Mart positions employees at the front door to greet people as they come into their store. They want their customers to feel they came to the right store and the employees are happy to serve them. I also noticed the same service at Cracker Barrel restaurants. When I walked through the door, a strong voice acknowledged me, saying "Welcome to Cracker Barrel." All of this suggests to me that there is power in greeting people the right way and making them feel good they came, resulting in them spending their resources and returning.

A good hospitality ministry is the key to membership retention. It is critical because in some churches, people leave as fast as they come, and in others, no one joins. The questions some churches need to ask are: "How do we retain the people God sends to our church? How do we keep new people coming in? How do we close the back door to prevent them from walking out?" Every church must have something to set it apart from the rest. Another good question we can ask as leaders is: Why should people pass one hundred other churches on Sunday morning and attend your service? I really believe hospitality is one of the key elements that will cause people to return.

Hospitality should be intentional and not taken lightly. It makes people feel wanted and like they matter. It gives people the feeling of family, making them feel they belong. Therefore, we must offer it with cheerful hearts because we want to make a difference in people's lives. Doing this helps us stay in alignment with the Word of God. It shows we are carrying out the principles found in the Word of God.

> You should be like one big happy family, full of sympathy toward each other, loving one another with tender hearts and humble minds. (1 Peter 3:8 TLB)

> Therefore, as God's chosen people, holy and dearly loved, clothe yourselves with compassion, kindness, humility, gentleness and patience. (Col. 3:12 NIV)

> Offer hospitality to one another without grumbling. (1 Peter 4:9 NIV)

When people see this kind of action in the church, it gets their attention, mainly when they are seeking the right place for membership.

There's no doubt the churches that excel in hospitality will be remembered. It is said that 85 percent of church growth comes out of hospitality or how we make people feel. Our goal for the hospitality program is to be a model for the entire church in proving people with the best in hospitality, both at the church and away from it. To make this happen, we were inspired with a new purpose, which is now written, for all hospitality workers to be trained. The purpose of our hospitality program is

> To ensure that every person who comes in contact with our church, by word of mouth or worship participation, will feel welcomed, accepted, comfortable, and valued in a way that will lead them to Christ and the church.

The Requirements for a Good Hospitality Ministry

Every church needs a cutting-edge hospitality ministry to make people feel welcome when they visit. It takes special people to do this work. As with any organization, hospitality ministries must be led by people who meet certain qualifications.

They Must Be Dependable

The church must be able to count on the hospitality workers. Inconsistent workers can really hurt the church because when people are used to receiving good service, they are disappointed when it stops, so we must continue providing it. If we stop, we may lose our worship crowd. We must be consistent in what we do.

They Must Be Available

The church must have hospitality workers who are available—people who have the time to serve in the ministry. The workers in this ministry cannot be so busy that they do not have time to serve. They must know they can't plan things on the days they are scheduled to serve. Some people are so busy with everything else that when they do show up to serve, they are still not really available because their minds are not on the work. They are not creative, and their warmth and giving presentation are totally out of focus. As a matter of fact, these people are the ones who covey less warmth during the service simply because they are not available.

They Must Be Credible

The church must be able to trust them. They must maintain a good report. People must be able to respect them as honest and caring people. If they greet people coming in, they must also greet them going out of the church. Hospitality allows people to use their gifts to help lead the church to a state of maturity. I believe we can apply the following Scriptures with the purpose of hospitality work:

> Why is it that he gives us these special abilities to do certain things best? It is that God's people will be equipped to do better work for him, building up the Church, the body of Christ, to a position of strength and maturity; until finally we all believe alike about our salvation and about our Savior, God's Son, and all become full-grown in the Lord—yes, to the point of being filled full with Christ. (Eph. 4:12–13 TLB)

Developing Hospitality Ministry Opportunities

Sometimes we rob people of an opportunity to serve in hospitality by keeping the ministry too narrow. We limit the ministry to only a few positions, such as ushering, nursing, and maybe a few greeters. In many churches, you only find ushers and nurses. I believe if we could be a little more creative, we would find many different hospitality opportunities for people to serve, which will keep them involved. It wouldn't hurt to stop and investigate how many hospitality opportunities are available in your church. It also wouldn't hurt us to ask a few questions when it comes to hospitality, like: What kind of hospitality ministries do we already have in place? Are they working? Is there anything else we can do to help close the back door?

At this point I want to share with you some of the hospitality opportunities formed in my spirit that work well at our church. They also work very well at other churches where I have presented workshops for their membership. Hospitality touches everyone and gives them hope. Therefore, we need to create as many opportunities as possible to serve. Here are three different categories of hospitality opportunities.

I. Parking Team Category

1. Traffic Directors

This team is placed at every entrance of the church. They direct traffic to the available parking areas. They wear the green or orange vests and use professional bright orange or red handheld batons as they direct the traffic. This team provides a great sense of care and amazement. They are secured with visible radios at all times.

2. Parking Attendants

This team assists with parking by identifying the next available parking spot in a particular parking section. They welcome the people with great enthusiasm and introduce them to a parking lot greeter, who walks them to the entrance door of the church where the entrance door host is waiting to receive them. This team also wears green vests and carries umbrellas to ensure no worshipper gets wet during inclement weather entering or leaving the service. This team is secured with visible radios.

II. Parking Lot Greeters Team Category

1. First-Time Guest Greeters

This team greets all first-time guests with great enthusiasm and bright smiles to give them a sense of hope and expectancy. This team walks them to the entrance door, where the entrance door host is waiting to receive them.

2. Outside-Membership Greeters Team

This team is placed throughout the parking lot to greet all the worshippers with a warm, friendly smile and walk them to the entrance door of the church, where the entrance door host is waiting to receive them.

III. Inside—the Building Greeters Team Category

1. Entrance Door Host

This team welcomes all members and guests to a great day of worship. They present all worshippers to the sanctuary greeter for proper seating. They connect all children with the children's church host, who guides them to their place of worship.

2. The Hallway Host

This team is positioned in the hallways throughout the church. They greet worshippers at various entrances into the church building and lead them to the sanctuary greeters. They also assist them with their coats to ensure comfort during worship.

3. The Sanctuary Greeter

This team balances the seating by directing the people to the floor usher who will seat and serve them. They ensure the church is filled equally according to sections to avoid empty spots in the seating arrangement.

4. The Floor Usher

This team receives, seat, and serves the worshippers throughout the worship service and assists them with information or anything they might need to make their worship experience a great one. They ensure the church is being filled from the front to the back so worshippers are not disturbed by people who are running late.

5. Utility Host

This team sits up front and monitors the seating. As the worship center fills up, they make arrangements to put out chairs in the least-distracting way possible and to serve as assistants to others, as needed.

6. Worship Nurses

This team provides water, handkerchiefs, or any other means of comfort for the pastor and worship leaders during the service so they might serve God and people during the worship experience.

7. Medical Team

This team provides medical assistance if necessary or contacts a medical professional in times of sickness during the worship service. This team serves all worship areas of the church.

8. Inside Security Team

This team monitors the hallway during worship service. They look for suspicious behaviors and are prepared to make a connection with city authorities if necessary. This team carries radios that are visible to the worshippers at all times.

9. Parking Security Team

As the people gather for worship, this team is seen riding in cars with security lights flashing to give the worshippers a sense of safety for their cars. This team secures the parking until the service is over; they also see the people back to their cars and thank them for coming. This team is secured with visible radios.

All teams must be available to greet and direct people as they depart the worship service. To not do this will make it look like a setup. People expect great things when they come, but they are really impressed by how we lead them out of the church. As you can see, this hospitality program is much bigger than just ushering and serving as church nurses. We created thirteen places for people to serve during worship service. Remember, everyone is touched by some form of hospitality and can be used somewhere. This approach to hospitality has been taught in the Wolverine State Congress of Christian Education and in churches seeking a new approach to ministry.

Chapter 8

The Shepherding Program

$\mathfrak{I}$ n this chapter, we will look at a program God gave me to help lead the church according to the direction of the vision. The name of this program is Shepherding. The purpose for this program is to ensure the church's vision pillars (intellectual, physical, spiritual, and social) are working effectively in the lives of every member of the church. This program is led by people with hearts for shepherding who I have trained and appointed to nurture the membership in spiritual growth, assume responsibility for their welfare, and teach and equip them for ministry. The expected outcome of this program is to help ease the burden of leadership by sharing the work with others. The idea was taken from Exodus 18, where Moses' father-in-law, Jethro, gave him instructions on how to lead the people God had placed in his care. Moses had a heavy burden caring for himself and the people and would suffer from exhaustion if changes were not made. The Scriptures say,

The next day Moses took his seat to serve as judge for the people, and they stood around him from morning till evening. When his father-in-law saw all that Moses was doing for the people, he said, "What is this you are doing for the people? Why do you alone sit as judge, while all these people stand around you from morning till evening?" Moses answered him, "Because the people come to me to seek God's will. Whenever they have a dispute, it is brought to me, and I decide between the parties and inform them of God's decrees and laws." Moses' father-in-law replied, "What you are doing is not good. You and these people who come to you will only wear yourselves out. The work is too heavy for you; you cannot handle it alone." (Ex. 18:13–18 NIV)

Moses' New Job Description

Following Jethro's constructive criticism, Moses received some God-sent advice to help save him and the people from overworking themselves and experiencing burnout. This wisdom is seen in these verses:

Listen now to me and I will give you some advice, and may God be with you. You must be the people's representative before God and bring their disputes to him. Teach them the decrees and laws, and show them the way to live and the duties they are to perform. (Ex. 18:19–20 NIV)

God always has someone who can get us back on track if we listen to his or her advice. Sometimes we as leaders suffer many hardships because we do not listen. I can attest to this, as I didn't always listen when I had a chance. As stated in chapter 2, God sent people to me who shared information that could have helped me tremendously, but I didn't listen to them.

Jethro said to Moses, "Listen and I will give you some advice." He said, "You must represent the people before God and bring their disputes to Him." In other words, as their representative, Moses was to bring their disagreements to God to be resolved. Moses was told to instruct them in the law and show them how to live by godly principles. These instructions can also help us today if we will listen. They will help us to become better leaders and to properly train future leaders for our congregations. In the very next verse, Moses was instructed to select men to help him lead the people. They had to be people who possessed certain characteristics.

The Shepherd's Qualification

> But select capable men from all the people—men who fear
> God, trustworthy men who hate dishonest gain—and appoint
> them as officials over thousands, hundreds, fifties and tens.
> (Ex. 18:21 NIV)

Jethro described to Moses what kind of people he must choose for leadership. First and foremost, they had to be capable men, meaning they must be competent, able, talented, skilled, and gifted to do the work. He said they must be people who fear God, meaning they must love God more than anything, respect Him highly, and honor Him with their whole hearts. Last but not least, he said they must be trustworthy, meaning people who are responsible, dependable, reliable, honest, and truthful. I know for a fact that over the years I struggled with this part by not getting the facts before I placed people in ministry.

If you recall from chapter 2, I learned this lesson the hard way when I appointed a person to be a trustee and he tried to turn the other trustees against me. Everything that looks good may not be good for the ministry. There used to be a time when, if a person left one church and joined another, the leader of the new church would question the former ministry to get information on whether the person would be a good investment for membership or certain ministries. I don't think too much follow up is being done in today's ministries—especially the smaller ones who are desperate for members. For this reason, smaller churches are more subject to being hurt.

Transferred growth can be dangerous if you don't know how to handle it or how to get the facts to protect the church. It is critical for leaders to take their time and prayerfully choose those who will help them in ministry because the outcome of the ministry depends heavily on these leadership characteristics. Our Shepherding ministry is based on these instructions Moses received, with a few additional qualifications.

The Shepherd Must Love God More than Anything

When it comes to loving God, the shepherd must represent it better than others, because people need an idea to follow in building a relationship with God. They need a role model who will demonstrate the love of God in his or her life, as the Scripture teaches,

> Love the Lord your God with all your heart and with all your soul and with all your mind. (Matt. 22:37 NIV)

This commandment speaks to all people who are following Christ. I believe it speaks first to the leaders of the church of God. To lead people in spiritual matters without loving God is contradictory to His Word. God must be first in every leader's life. He or she must love the Lord more than anything. To love God is to worship Him, and to worship

God is to love Him. Loving God with your all is to surrender everything to Him as it relates to your time, talent, resources, and being. The leader's task is to guide people to love God in this fashion.

The Shepherd Must Speak the Language of the Pastor

God uses the example of a nation engaged in disobedience to show us the power of people speaking the same language. Genesis 11:1–5 describes how the people were trying to go to heaven their own way, without being obedient to God. Even though they took the wrong approach, the power of their unity led the Lord to come down to earth and put a stop to their efforts. Listen to what God had to say about them.

> The Lord said, "If as one people speaking the same language
> they have begun to do this, then nothing they plan to do will
> be impossible for them. (Gen. 11:6 NIV)

When people are on the same page, operating in one thought and purpose, nothing can stop them. The leadership and the pastor of the church must walk together in harmony and be in one accord. When this happens, nothing can stop them from reaching the levels before them. Unity is what connects us with God and releases His presence among us. Jesus said,

> Again, I tell you that if two of you on earth agree about
> anything you ask for, it will be done for you by my Father in
> heaven. For where two or three come together in my name,
> there am I with them. (Matt. 18:19–20 NIV)

The Shepherd Must Catch Vision Quickly

If it takes too long for the leader to understand the direction the pastor is leading, one or two things may be wrong: either the pastor isn't clear in his articulation of the vision or the leader is sluggish in his or her understanding of the vision. It suggests he or she may not be ready for the task of leading a group of people. The evidence of not catching the vision quickly is procrastination, half-heartedness, or slow performance. In some cases, by the time the leader actually catches the vision, the vision work will already be outdated. A great sign of catching vision is seen in this verse:

> After Paul had seen the vision, we got ready at once to leave
> for Macedonia, concluding that God had called us to preach
> the gospel to them. (Acts 16:10 NIV)

Leaders have to be able to move when it's time to move. A vision that comes from the Lord to the pastor cannot be controlled by those who cannot see it. Luke said in the above verse that after Paul had seen the vision, "We got ready at once." (In between seeing the vision and them getting ready, Paul had to articulate the vision clearly to them.) They got ready at once, with no signs of procrastination, to go to Macedonia, concluding that the Lord had called them to preach the gospel to the Macedonians. This means they were totally convinced and had no doubt in their minds. They caught the vision, understood it, and were ready to apply it. These are the kind of leaders who can help grow great churches for God.

The Shepherd Must Lead with Integrity

> Keep watch over yourselves and all the flock of which
> the Holy Spirit has made you overseers. Be shepherds of

the church of God, which he bought with his own blood.
(Acts 20:28 NIV)

I pass this Scripture on to every leader I train in ministry because when I delegate ministry into the hands of leaders, I am sharing the work God called me to perform. Along with the work comes a call to lead with integrity, which is demanded of every leader. All leaders should fall under these instructions because leadership like this will keep the group or church healthy. The shepherd leader is not the pastor; shepherd leaders help the pastor oversee the flock.

The Responsibilities of the Shepherd

And appoint them as officials over thousands, hundreds, fifties and tens. Have them serve as judges for the people at all times, but have them bring every difficult case to you; the simple cases they can decide themselves. That will make your load lighter, because they will share it with you. If you do this and God so commands, you will be able to stand the strain, and all these people will go home satisfied. (Ex. 18:21–23 NIV)

From this passage, we learn the responsibility of the shepherd. It describes what the leaders are to do as helpers to the pastor. There are specific assignments given, and if they are carried out properly, they will help the pastor withstand the strain of leading a large group of people. Their assignment is to serve as officials or group leaders over the number of people they have the ability to lead. Everyone can't lead the same number of people. A person who can only lead ten people should not be given fifty people to lead. If this happens, the group of fifty will soon become a group of ten, as that is all the leader can handle; the rest will leave due to a lack of care. There is nothing wrong with the leader if he can only handle ten. It's just a reflection of his God-given ability to lead.

In their individual groups, the appointed leaders had the task of judging between right and wrong and listening to the cry of the people so Moses didn't have to be burdened with every little complaints or issue, which drained him of his energy to lead. The leaders were instructed to handle the small cases and report the tough ones to Moses. In leadership, there are some things only the pastor should handle. Every leader must know what to take to the pastor and what to handle on his or her own. In this way, leaders will be sharing the work with the pastor in a more efficient way, which makes his work load lighter as he labors to serve the people. This is the secret of leadership longevity.

Other Responsibilities of the Shepherd

When helping the pastor lead the flock, there are other responsibilities the shepherd leader must fulfill. He or she must cast the vision for the group. A good leader understands what the pastor asks of him or her and has things in place by the time he needs it. This is a perfect example of catching the vision and running with it.

The only work shepherd leaders have to do is the work that has already been ordered by the Holy Spirit for the senior pastor. They are to be trained and taught in the work at hand and to be creative in developing it. If leaders aren't doing what they were put in position to do, you can't help but wonder what they are doing with the people. Every pastor should know his or her vision well enough to be able to tell when something strange is going on. The senior pastor makes the assignments for all of his leaders and allows them to use their own personalities, creativity, and judgment to make it happen so they can have a significant place in the work. But it must be done according to the vision of the senior pastor.

The shepherd leader should also be trained and ready to serve communion to the people in his or her group and to visit the sick who are in the hospital or shut in at home with the company of another person. The pastor will take care of the sick calls from those who are critical. These leaders also assist in the bereavement cases by calling, sending cards, and taking food to bereaved families' homes while the pastor handles the funeral preparations, officiates the service, and gives the message for the deceased people's families.

The Shepherd's Task

The shepherd's task is to ensure several things as they relate to building the body of Christ and the church. The tasks are as follows.

The Shepherd Must Build an Effective Leadership Team

The shepherd must build a team equipped to help lead the groups. This team is designed to ensure the shepherd is multiplying himself through teaching, training, and leading. At New Life, every shepherd leader has a six-member leadership team called purpose leaders, who also help direct the groups according to the vision pillars of the church. Every shepherd must have an assistant and every purpose leader must have a qualified assistant, so when the group becomes too large, there is already leadership in place to start another class. In developing the leadership for the vision pillars, I used the four purposes Rick Warren wrote about in his book called *The Purpose-Driven Church*[6] to help build and set the direction of the leadership. I incorporated them into the four pillars God gave me. This work is seen in the purpose leader's job description.

---

6   Rick Warren, *The Purpose-Driven Church*. (Grand Rapids,

   MI: Zondervan Publishing House, 1995).

The Intellectual/Discipleship Development Purpose Leader:
This purpose leader works with the shepherd leader to ensure intellectual development within the group by keeping it growing through principles from the Word. This purpose leader focuses on Bible study activities, attendance, giving, and providing intellectual development speeches to keep the class or group motivated.

The Physical Development Purpose Leader: This purpose leader works with the shepherd leader to ensure physical development within the group by doing things to keep the people healthy and making sure each member is involved in healthy activities. This purpose leader focuses on planning aerobics activities, walking activities, nutritional programs, and physical development motivational speeches.

The Spiritual/Worship Development Purpose Leader: This purpose leader works with the shepherd leader in securing worship participation to ensure the group is growing stronger. This purpose leader focuses on keeping the students involved in attending prayer sessions, participating in a weekly worship to God, posting Scripture readings and thoughts on a social networking site for the members' encouragement, and making motivational spiritual development speeches to keep the group on fire for Christ and the church.

The Social Development Purpose Leaders: There are three growth components that make up this pillar, and each has its own purpose leader to ensure its development:

The Fellowship Purpose Leader: This purpose leader's focus is on building relationships within the group. He or she creates fellowship activities to keep the group growing warmer by organizing food fellowships during the year for the group members and their families for the purpose of strengthening the bond of the group. This leader focuses on Sunday school attendance, ensuring every person is involved in sharing his or her life with the group. This leader also communicates with new members who join the group and encourages them to complete the new members' class and provide motivational speeches when necessary.

The Ministry Purpose Leader: This purpose leader works with the shepherd leader in ensuring ministry involvement within the group to make certain the church is growing broader. This leader's focus is on making sure all group members are involved in ministry. They also plan quarterly community service work to get the group outside of the church walls and make motivational speeches when needed.

The Evangelistic Purpose Leader: This purpose leader works with the shepherd leader to ensure the group is growing larger. This leader focuses on planning one or two evangelistic food fellowship events annually to serve as a bridge to lead group member's neighbors, friends, coworkers, schoolmates, relatives, and anyone else they want to see go to heaven into the church. This leader's task is to see that people are being saved and make motivational speeches to the group when necessary.

Together these six purpose leaders work with the shepherd leaders to help their group members grow to be spiritually healthy believers who together might effect change in the church community and world. The vision the Lord gave us in chapter 3 would be less effective without people standing at the foot of it, praying and doing the things necessary to make it reality. Our shepherding team is a visionary group of people who have caught the vision and are making it happen through prayer and commitment. Working together, they see the results of Scripture in their leadership.

> Two are better than one, because they have a good return for their work: If one falls down, his friend can help him up. But pity the man who falls and has no one to help him up! Also, if two lie down together, they will keep warm. But how can one keep warm alone? Though one may be overpowered, two can defend themselves. A cord of three strands is not quickly broken. (Eccles. 4:9–12 NIV)

The Shepherd Builds a Great Sunday School Department (LDH)

The shepherd and his leadership team lead the church in age-appropriate groups that make up our Sunday school, better known as our Life Development Groups. We changed the name of our Sunday school to give people a new look at what we are trying to do. I know many people today look at Sunday school as if it is for children only. It is for this reason the Sunday school ministry in many churches never exceeds thirty students in participation. We changed our name to Life Development Hour (LDH), meaning this is a time we spend together sharing and learning from each other's life experiences as we focus on Scripture.

We motivate people in these age groups according to the vision and direction in which the Holy Spirit is leading the church. The classes are held at the same time (9:30 a.m.) each Sunday morning and are held in houses we purchased and renovated in the community. Our goal is to create the concept in Acts 2 about moving people from house to house with a sense of unity in the community. This program has been amazingly effective in getting the attention of the community and has even stopped traffic on Sunday mornings. Imagine more than two hundred people walking from their community small group houses from all directions to gather for worship at the worship center.

The focus of the group leaders is on building relationships and making people feel like family. Our ultimate goal is to lead them into a family they have never had and to find friendships they have never encountered. In our various settings, we share our lives and pray for those who may be going through difficult situations.

We encourage group members to protect what people share in the groups at all times so the group will always be a safe place for people to release and share their life experiences. We aim to keep the groups small enough to learn and allow time for everyone to be heard. Our groups are arranged in age groups of: thirteen to fifteen, sixteen to eighteen, nineteen to twenty-four, twenty-five to thirty-one, thirty-two to thirty-seven, thirty-eight to forty-six, forty-seven to fifty-two, fifty-three to fifty-eight, fifty-nine to sixty-five, and sixty-six and up. As the group members reach certain ages, they are promoted to another age group to learn and share at another level of maturity and to experience new relationships. When a group is too large, we start another group. The secret is to multiply each group every year and to have leadership ready for each new group.

Our goal is to not have a Bible study during this time. We get our Bible study in a different setting. The small-group discussions are based on my message from week to week. A sermon outline is passed out every week so the leader and students can take notes and be prepared to ask questions and share in the class discussion. I believe the message the Spirit gives me for Sunday morning is what the church should be focusing on for their lives. Therefore, all shepherd leaders are instructed to take good notes on the sermon, seek to feel my heart for the people as I preach, and hear where Holy Spirit is taking us with the message so they can create questions to lead a group discussion related to the message. We change the study material from time to time to keep the groups growing deeper into the Word of God.

Every lesson is led with questions phrased to guide students to the answer the leaders want to hear. This helps the leader to know if the students are really benefiting from the sermons or lessons given. This learning tool also helps the leaders to be aware of problem areas in the students' lives that might need ministering to. Teaching from the pastor's message also gives more people an opportunity to share in the development of other people's lives. The shepherd leaders don't have to be Bible scholars to lead these discussions because the pastor does the research and gives the Scripture base. All the leaders are challenged to find and use other appropriate Scriptures that help reinforce the original lesson. The idea of studying the Bible on their own helps keep them sharp in the Word.

We filter everything through our LDH groups. When we need workers in any area of ministry in the church, we look for them through the groups. Before we start new ministries, we look to the LDH groups for workers. I teach all new members who join our church that if we can't get them to LDH, the chances are they will not be committed to church for very long. People who don't attend Life Development Hour often don't ever feel like family and never build great relationships because they don't attend the sessions designed to make it happen. If people attend LDH, you can count on them to be your best help in the church.

I found out that there are many benefits to having a strong Sunday school (LDH) department. Being in LDH solves a lot of potential problems on Sunday morning. If the people are in LDH, they are unlikely to be late for worship service. They will also be more focused for worship, and the chances of them changing their minds about church will be few. Think about this: if you can have two hundred people in Sunday school (LDH), you are likely to start your worship service with two hundred people. This is much better than what you'll have otherwise, because everyone is on time and able to share in the singing at the beginning of service.

He Oversees the Roll Call Attendance of the Group

Most leaders like working with people. They love leading classroom discussions or teaching the lesson for the day, but not too many like the administrative part of leadership, like keeping roll call. A good leader studies the numerical health of the group by keeping track of who's present, who's absent, who's late, who is attending, and who is not attending at all. The shepherd and his team catch this before it is too far gone by studying the weekly roll call.

A good roll call can prevent losing members if you keep your eyes on the student's group participation. The fact is if we care, then we will be aware of what is going on with the people we are leading. The social/fellowship purpose leader oversees these areas while the intellectual/ discipleship purpose leaders take care of mid-week attendance. All new members are added to the roll call so they can be encouraged to be part of the Life Development Hour and Bible study. *An example of the roll call can be seen in appendix III.*

He Oversees the Yearly Income Budget

We set our budgets through LDH. These are the people we can trust to honor their financial commitments to Christ and the church. This is why the Sunday school department (or whatever name you choose to call it) needs to be large in attendance. They represent not only the ministry workers and volunteers of the church, but they are also your best financial supporters. We hand out a financial giving commitment card every year for the students to complete and return since they know what their tithes, offerings, and Sunday school offerings or mid-offerings are better than anyone. The students write what they plan to give on the card, and we pass it on to the trustees, who use the card to determine the church budget for the year. This information helps keep the integrity of the membership in place.

There's nothing better than knowing you can count on the members of your church when it comes to giving. This program really helps a pastor know who can be counted on. The card lists all the areas of giving, and the annual budget is produced by calculating each member's stated financial commitment. For example, let's say a person indicates his or her tithes will be $50 per week; we multiply the amount of their tithes by fifty-two weeks to calculate his or her total tithes for the year. We do the same calculation for each area of giving and add them up for each category, and this gives us our yearly budget. The shepherd is taught how to process the cards from his group to produce the giving strength of his group. I believe this idea will work well for smaller churches who are laying a foundation to grow larger. Please see our age group yearly income *commitment card in appendix IV.*

He Oversees the Weekly Financial Reports

The financial numbers are processed from the yearly budget commitment card and placed on a monthly giving worksheet whereby the shepherd leaders monitor their age groups every week to see their financial health. By watching the giving habits weekly, you will be able to see who is faithful, who has fallen off, and who has stopped giving. Usually when faithful members stop giving, it didn't just start or happen overnight.

When faithful members stop giving, it usually began as a process. People stop giving a little at a time. First they start missing a little at a time, a week here, a week there, and then they move to a couple of weeks here and there. Their giving follows the same pattern, and from there they gradually stop attending. The next thing you know, both the person and his or her money are gone. A good financial worksheet will help the shepherds keep their groups financially healthy. I suggest if you are considering doing this that you take the time to produce your own spreadsheet according to the direction of the church. The main idea is the leadership needs to know what is going on in this most important area of growth with the group.

He Attends Monthly Evaluation Accountability Meetings

The shepherd meets monthly with the senior pastor to discuss the health of his or her group. The focus is on LDH and Bible study roll calls, the financial stability of the group, and making sure people are involved in ministry and soul winning. Our goal is for every group to grow, and if growth is not taking place in these areas, we know something is hindering it. It could be outside forces, membership problems, or leadership problems.

If the income or attendance is down for the group, we try to identify the cause. It could be the people are no longer working, income has been cut for some reason, or people are just losing interest in the group. Maybe we need to find a way to assist them in their needs rather than looking for them to give. If all is well at the accountability meeting, the leader returns to the group and celebrates the group's accomplishments. However, if the members are not keeping their financial or attendance commitments, then the shepherd must address the situation. This is the tough part of ministry that many people don't want to deal with. If the finances in a group are lagging and the shepherd is afraid to talk about it because he or she is afraid of hurting the person's feelings, then the Devil has a hold on that shepherd, because he knows blessings are connected with giving that we can't get unless we are committed to giving. The Word of God supports this.

> Give, and it will be given to you. A good measure, pressed down, shaken together and running over, will be poured into your lap. For with the measure you use, it will be measured to you. (Luke 6:38 NIV)

It is critical for the shepherd leader to challenge the students to give by showing them the benefits that come with giving, just as he show the benefits that come with studying the Word, caring for the body, worshipping God, building relationships, serving in ministry, and winning the lost to Christ.

I have heard many times from preachers and teachers of the Word of God that Christ wants us to ask so He can give, He wants to give so we can have, and He wants us to have so we can be happy. He wants us to be happy because happiness is the greatest form of advertisement for the kingdom of God. This is a good reason why people should give. As leaders, we must be ready to give motivational speeches to our groups to keep them trusting God through their giving and their commitment to attendance and serving in ministry.

The Shepherd and Purpose Leader

Evangelistic Drive That Ends In Worship

This program is led by the shepherd and purpose leaders. It is a church-wide attempt to work together, regardless of age, to connect people to

Christ and the church. We believe it will attract hundreds of souls and ensure souls are getting on the church radar. It starts on the outside and ends up on the inside. This evangelistic drive will connect with the lost and bring them to a worship service through those who did the inviting. This program deals with a three-month evangelistic drive four times a year. There are certain things taking place during this drive that can attract the people you are trying to reach. They will think about your church when they are ready to make a decision for Christ. If they decide to join another church, you will have done your job, and God will still be pleased.

This drive gets the entire church involved in the mission of the church. It presents you with more than one chance to minister to the people you are trying to reach, should you fail during the process. This drive will also give you a chance to change bait if what you are using is not working. Through this program, we cast our nets for three months and draw the lost in on the fifth Sunday by inviting them to a worship service designed to help them make a decision for Christ.

The reason we miss out on winning many souls for Christ and the church is because we don't use enough strategies to connect people to Christ. God has already given us tools to work with, and many of us haven't given any thought on how to use them to win souls. Whatever the vision is for the church, there is something in the vision to help you connect with the lost because this is the main purpose for vision. If your vision can't help you connect with lost souls, then the vision must not be inspired by God. A good vision directs everything we do with the church and helps us reach the unconnected in the community. Vision births new ideas for evangelism and ministry. I have learned that we must have new paradigms that serve as a tool for Christ to do a new thing in our church.

We are using our four pillars to create this evangelistic drive. The vision gave birth to these pillars I discussed in chapter 3. The pillars of intellectual, physical, spiritual and social development also became the top four core values of our church to help us stay focused on the vision. These pillars are being used as an evangelistic instrument to bring many to Christ and the church. Every three months, a different pillar is giving direction to what we need to do in the community to draw people into the house of worship.

I'm hoping the readers of this chapter will focus on the simplicity of the approach and perhaps look for ways they can use the information in their ministries. I also hope, above all, that this chapter will help them bring many people into the church that they might see, fear, and put their trust in God. It is to this end I will give the direction of each vision pillars—intellectual, physical, spiritual, and social development—as they relate to an evangelistic drive planned to bring many to Christ and the church.

The Intellectual Pillar Worship Sunday

The first quarter of the year is committed to the intellectual development pillar. During this period, we promote education. We spend time in the school system walking the halls, showing the students we care about their learning. We talk to college students who are friends with our members as we see them and encourage them to excel. At the end of the three-month drive, we close it with a powerful worship service where we invite all the people we have communicated with over the past three months. The entire worship service is built around education and learning. We invite every sorority and fraternity organization we know, along with every schoolteacher or professor who can attend the special educational promotion weekend worship service. We expect the house to be filled with un-churched people, along with people who are churched. We believe if we do our homework and the legwork, the

Holy Spirit will send the people. I believe we ought to use every tool and connection Christ has given us to promote the Great Commission of Jesus Christ.

The Physical Pillar Worship Sunday

The second quarter of the year is committed to the physical development pillar. When it comes to physical fitness, I have discovered we all have a lot in common. We push everything we can think of that relates to caring for our bodies. We invite our un-churched friends, coworkers, neighbors, and associates to walk with us on the quarter-mile track. Those who can play basketball invite their friends to play with them.

We promote nutrition during these months, encouraging people to eat healthy and to maintain good balance with their weight. While dieting, we encourage them to focus on all four pillars as they eat cabbage soup, vegetables, and fruit and to pray that God will increase their knowledge and give them strength as it pertains to intellectual, physical, spiritual, and social development. We invite our friends and others to share with us in our prayer fast diet and to use our suggested meal plan to maintain good eating habits. At the end of the three-month drive, we close with a healthy-is-wealthy fitness promotion weekend. On Saturday we host a health fair, and on Sunday we promote health in worship.

During the time of the health fair and worship, some people are dressed in our "Healthy is Wealthy" fitness T-shirt, promoting good health. We decorate the fellowship hall with health pictures, and during our health expo, we show exercise videos to get the attendees motivated. We also put out a table at the expo to share health information that our partners produced to assist the people with their health concerns.

On Sunday, the church is decorated with fitness posters and banners to promote healthy living. Before and after service, we provide a meal consisting of fruit and other healthy food choices. Video clips are shown during worship service of people who have lost weight from dieting and exercising. The people also share how the plan God has given our church helped them manage their weight and eating habits. We even make our opening song an exercise song by ensuring the song is fast paced, which allows people to get involved in the service. We also let everyone know we are preparing for worship by getting rid of all pain through movement to the opening song. This time together is so much fun as we prepare to worship God later into the service. On this day, I pray for God to give me a message to promote physical development and show people we are a ministry for the whole person and that we, as a church, care about our health as we promote the Word of God.

> Dear friend, I pray that you may enjoy good health and that all may go well with you, even as your soul is getting along well. (3 John 1:2 NIV)

The Spiritual Pillar Worship Sunday

For three months, our focus is on the spiritual pillar. Our focus for this time is on hearing the Word of God and talking to God through prayer. We pass out prayer request forms every week and encourage people to fill them out with their prayer requests. We take the forms into the community, work, and school and encourage people to fill them out and let our prayer team pray for them. We encourage them to let us pray for their sick who may be in the hospital. We make sure they include their names and addresses on the form so we can invite them to our spiritual pillar worship service.

On the day of the spiritual pillar worship service, we plan the biggest event of the quarter to make an impact in their lives. We sing songs we know everyone can relate to, and we make sure every song has the right flavor to touch the heart. We include a worship dance designed to lead people to sense the presence of God; we execute the flags and strings to capture the soul, heart, and mind in the glory of God, and we make worship current and relevant, using media to give people what they can't get anywhere else.

The Social Pillar Worship Sunday

For three months, our focus is on the social pillar, where we push fellowship, ministry, and evangelism. For fellowship, we host a community picnic. All members are encouraged to invite all of their unconnected family members to introduce them to their spiritual family. We want them to know who we are and that Christian fellowship is not all bad and to show them we know how to have fun together. We also want them to know we care.

For the ministry pillar, the whole church is encouraged to engage in a community clean-up project. We find a piece of property we would like to own for our ministry and that is in need of care. We cut the grass, clean up the site, and make the piece of property look good in the community. The church makes a big service day out of the project and asks the members to bring their lawnmowers, rakes, and cutting shears to help beautify the property and community. The project is well-organized for maximum community impact. We also call in the media on this day to make a community statement to the public.

We intentionally talk to passers-by and people who show interest in what we are doing. We pass out information about our mission and about our church ministries and how they can help us make a life-changing difference. We invite them to attend our church services and to use our recreational facility for their benefit. We eat lunch together and invite neighbors to share with us during our mealtime. On Saturday before the social pillar worship, we host a big community household giveaway. The members of the church invite people they know who need help to attend a special service where we talk about the difference Christ can make in their lives. After the service, they take their guests and help them find some free household items. The giveaway is done outside in the park.

On the closing Sunday for this quarter, we plan the biggest social development worship service we can to make a difference in the community. As an evangelistic attempt, we invite all the people we made contact with during this drive to worship with us and hope we have pleased God and impacted their lives in a way that will prompt them to accept Christ as their Savior and return and become a member of the church. *This program was endorsed by Dr. Addis Moore, the president of Wolverine State Baptist Congress of Christian Education. Please read appendix V.*

Chapter 9

From Parking Lots to Community

It was with great anticipation we waited for the Holy Spirit to move in a big way for the church. After putting things in order, we thought the Lord would increase our membership and expand our sanctuary for a larger worship attendance. With the vision and a new direction for the church, mission, and structure now in place I thought we were ready, but I was wrong again. God had a different idea for His work, and His thoughts were truly different than mine, as the Scripture teaches,

> For my thoughts are not your thoughts, neither are your ways
> my ways," declares the Lord. (Isa. 55:8 NIV)

He illuminated my mind to help me understand by asking me two questions. He said, "Do you need another sanctuary right now?" and

"Wouldn't it be better to build something for the community?" All my heart could say at this point was, "Yes, Lord!" Instantly I caught the vision and direction God wanted me to go with the church. He pointed out to me how people were suffering from a lack of community activities, programs, and a safe place to hold them. I got busy drawing up the idea and plans for a community one-stop building that would house community programs designed to meet intellectual, physical, spiritual, and social needs. We had it drawn to scale by an architect, only to find out the cost of the building was way out of our league at the time.

The building itself was equipped with a full-size gymnasium, an exercise room, a Jazz café, a commercial kitchen, a walking track, a library, a police mini-station, and an arcade . There would also be a beauty and barber shop, classrooms, a prayer room, a conference-banquet room, a pool hall, and much more to meet the needs of the community. The cost of this building would have been seven million dollars. I consulted God, and He made known to me what was happening. He revealed to me it was not the appointed time to build, which reminds me again of what the Scripture teaches,

> We should make plans—counting on God to direct us.
> (Prov. 16:9 TLB)

God showed me the building for motivational purposes. It turned out that God was preparing me for what was going to happen, which pertained to the first steps of His plans for the church. What God wanted first was for me to build a certain kind of team from within the church who would serve as a core group for the task ahead. I was instructed through the Holy Spirit to begin working on developing a three hundred solid soldiers team of people who would stand firm with me in what God wanted done.

This team was from among the members of the life-development groups of the church. In developing this team, I designed lessons for the leaders of the groups to help me with the training. They used the Word of God to motivate the people as we produced things to keep them inspired. Together we made tote bags, caps, and T-shirts all bearing the name three hundred solid solider team. The leadership team and their group members wore their special gear everywhere. We even wrote a song and sang it during special times in our worship service, called, "Do You Want to Be a Solid Solider for Christ?" The song reminded us of the requirements to be a solid solider.

The idea for this team came from Judges 7 where God called Gideon to win a war against 135,000 Midianites with only a few trained men. This story teaches us what God can do through a few people if they put their trust in Him. It also teaches us as leaders that we will not always have the full support of everyone around us in what God wants to do through us.

The story encourages believers by revealing God's divine strategy when the odds are against them. Using this story, I motivated the members of our life-development groups to walk with me as I followed Spirit's lead to develop one of the biggest community projects to ever take place through a church in our city—a city where blight and dilapidated houses had taken over and crime was at an all-time high. Our city was once classified as one of the most dangerous cities in the United States in 2003. In the midst of this, God called me to develop a three hundred solid solider team of people who would stand with me to the end.

At this point, I will give more details on the development of this team by focusing on the story of Gideon and how God gave them the victory. We will begin this victorious journey with what I call God's elimination process, and then we will look at the three qualifiers for the win.

God's Elimination Process

> Announce now to the people, "Anyone who trembles with fear
> may turn back and Leave Mount Gilead." So twenty-two thousand
> men left, while ten thousand remained. (Judges 7:3 NIV)

Gideon started with thirty-two thousand, and being obedient to the call of God, he let twenty-two thousand people leave without trying to stop them. This is where we get lost when it comes to our membership. We want to believe more is better, and if we lose people, we think we are going to be unsuccessful. Really more is better when we need more to get the job done, but more can also be damaging if they are not ready for the task.

God used a different kind of strategy to produce the team Gideon needed to win the battle. I believe I could call this strategy divine mathematics, which is a process that only God can work to perfection. The departure of the twenty-two thousand people left Gideon with only ten thousand people to handle a task most people would have written off as a lost cause. Gideon didn't complain. He just followed God's directions, which is the key to getting things done. We have to keep in mind that it's God's work, and the work has to be done His way and the results belong to Him.

After the twenty-two thousand left, God told Gideon he still had too many people and that He would have to sift them for him. God made it perfectly clear to Gideon that He, not Gideon, would call the shots in the separation He was about to make. I understand this based on experience; it is so easy for us to let the right one go and hold on to the wrong one. Many times we try to hold on to people God has already released from our ministries, and when this happens, we have even more troubles.

I remember when I did all I could to hold on to people because I only had a few left, and all it did was give people the wrong impression about the ministry, thinking that it couldn't survive without them. I once met with a great guy who joined our church to talk about our next steps together, only to discover he was bitter toward me because another person (who didn't get what he wanted as a staff member) spoke negatively about me to him, and we lost the entire family. If I had followed instructions as God had spoken, I believe we would have saved that family. With this in mind, I want to look at Gideon's challenge.

> But the Lord said to Gideon, "There are still too many men.
> Take them down to the water, and I will sift them for you there.
> If I say, 'This one shall go with you,' he shall go; but if I say, 'This
> one shall not go with you,' he shall not go." (Judges 7:4 NIV)

God told Gideon what to do as He made the separation so Gideon would know who his real warriors were. Many times we fail to get things done in big ways because we assume we have something but we really don't. It helps when you know you have people you can count on to get things done. God had a unique way of showing Gideon who would work faithfully with him.

When God finished, Gideon had a team of only three hundred committed soldiers who would stand with him against the 135,000. They were not just any three hundred people; they were three hundred loyal soldiers who were willing to let God qualify and equip them to do extraordinary things. This team didn't just win the war; there were three special things that qualified them to win.

They Were Approved by God

> So Gideon took the men down to the water. There the Lord
> told him, "Separate those who lap the water with their tongues
> like a dog from those who kneel down to drink." Three
> hundred men lapped with their hands to their mouths. All the
> rest got down on their knees to drink. (Judges 7:5–6 NIV)

Gideon was under direct orders from God to do exactly what He told him to do. As leaders, we need to know everyone is not going to fit into our ministry and allow God to make the adjustments. God is the only one who knows the heart of people and what they are thinking, more than the people themselves. Gideon made the right choice and did exactly what God commanded of him.

The test God gave was unique. I believe He called it this way because the ones who lapped with their hands could drink and watch for the enemy at the same time. You can't see the enemy if you are looking down. The ones drinking from their hands were proven by God to be dependable, trustworthy, reliable, unyielding, and enduring. After this test, Gideon sent 9,700 more men home, leaving him with only three hundred soldiers to fight against an army of 135,000. The odds were nearly 450 to 1, but Gideon and his three hundred soldiers still won the battle. The truth is this, when a few people get together, with transformed hearts they can upset history. They can change lives and change the world.

The members of our church needed this lesson because the work God was about to do through us wasn't going to make sense to outsiders, and I knew the naysayers would try to crush our efforts. Many people didn't want to see anything good happen in the neighborhood around our church, so the members needed to know when God approves you, nothing can stop the progress. The second thing that qualified them to win was that they obeyed leadership.

They Obeyed Leadership

What people have to understand when it comes to the Holy Spirit using them is there is no substitute for obedience. There is no alternative other than doing what the Spirit says. When God wants to do something that seems impossible to man, He speaks the faith into His chosen leader, and the leader then summons the people to follow as he articulates the direction God has given him. You have to do what God is leading you to do through the leadership at hand. This is important because when the marching orders are given, it only takes one disobedient person to derail the whole project. Let's look at how God orchestrated this plan of success.

Dividing the three hundred men into three companies, he placed trumpets and empty jars in the hands of all of them, with torches inside. (Judges 7:16 NIV)

I know someone today would have thought they had a better way to fight this battle because from a natural point of view, it just doesn't seem to be enough men to win the battle. Think about it; a team of three hundred, a trumpet, and empty jars with torches inside of them to fight against 135,000 people. Gideon was very confident at this point, and he gave them the secret for success in the following verses:

"Watch me," he told them. "Follow my lead. When I get to the edge of the camp, do exactly as I do. When I and all who are with me blow our trumpets, then from all around the camp blow yours and shout, 'For the Lord and for Gideon.'" (Judges 7:17–18 NIV)

Sometimes victory is like a science because it has to be produced in unusual ways. Notice Gideon gave the group sound advice; he said, "Watch me. Follow my lead, and do exactly as I do." The victory was in the direction God had already given. Obedience was the key to making it all a reality. When Gideon gave the orders, the three companies blew their trumpets and smashed the jars. Grasping the torches in their left hands and holding in their right hands the trumpets, they were to blow and shout,

A sword for the Lord and for Gideon! (Judges 7:20 NIV)

This strategy may not make sense to the natural man, but faith is about obedience, not what seems to make sense. The third thing that qualified them to win was that they held their positions.

They Held Their Positions

This may seem too simple to use as proof for victory, but the Bible notes that they held their positions. I have learned over the years that some churches are not successful because they don't hold their positions in what they are inspired to do. Many times we give up too soon and move on to something else because we think things are not going to happen. The only danger in doing this is you don't know how close you are to what you have worked so hard for. The Word of God shows us again what can happen if we don't stop.

Let us not become weary in doing good, for at the proper time we will reap a harvest if we do not give up. (Gal. 6:9 NIV)

Holding our positions is to keep following the direction we were given. If we do it long enough, we will have incredible success stories, but we have to be consistent in what we do. This is one reason why it takes small churches so long to grow in numbers. To grow a large church, the members have to be consistent in their attendance and fellowship. They have to hold firm their position in attendance and in their giving and other commitments.

This can also be applied to spiritual growth. Large Bible studies will never happen until the members hold their positions in attendance. This Scripture reveals the power of people holding their positions.

> While each man held his position around the camp, all the Midianites ran, crying out as they fled, When the three hundred trumpets sounded, the Lord caused the men throughout the camp to turn on each other with their swords. (Judges 7:21–22 NIV)

This is how the Israelites were so successful in winning the victory when the odds were against them. It was this lesson I used to build a team of people who would help me do what God wanted done. I needed a team who would hold their position and not run—a team who would stand with me to make a difference in the church, the community, and the world. I needed people who were determined to stick it out through the thick and thin and would keep moving forward through any kind of storm. I needed people who would put vision and dreams into action—a team that valued the Word of God. You can't run a community program without these kinds of people.

Dr. Reginald G. Flynn confirms this in his *book So You Think Your Church Isn't Big Enough*. He said,

> Pastors, words without action, we know, are meaningless rhetoric! It is my hope pastors will not only speak about the power of God's word, but lead their churches to operate in the power of God's word to transform impoverished communities and empower powerless people.[7]

---

7   G. Reginald Flynn, *So You Think Your Church Isn't Big Enough*. (New York: Triumph Publishing, 2010), 91.

These commitments would help us to become a three hundred–member team equipped to make great things happen. Along with the above three qualifiers to win the war, our team was challenged with six additional qualifiers that will equip us for success as we build a church for the community.

Commitment One: Life Development Hour

This is a commitment to attend the Life Development Hour (Sunday School) weekly to share their lives with other members and guests to build them up, support them in their struggles, and comfort them in times of trouble. What I discovered over the years is no matter how many people join the church, if they didn't commit to the LDH groups on Sunday morning, they wouldn't last long as members. If the new members don't make an attempt to share or develop their lives through the LDH groups, they will soon leave the church because they never developed any lasting relationships with the people who make up the small group church family. Sitting in the pews on Sunday isn't enough to keep one motivated to continue over the long haul. One must have relationships. In our LDH groups, we focus on what the Scripture teaches,

> Each of you should look not only to your own interests, but
> also to the interests of others. (Phil. 2:4 NIV)

When we meet together during this special time of development, we share our lives and support each other by listening and giving encouragement. One thing is certain: the church will not have a significant impact in the community until we first learn how to trust, encourage, and get along with one another, as the Scripture teaches us,

Let us not give up meeting together, as some are in the habit of doing, but let us encourage one another—and all the more as you see the Day approaching. (Heb. 10:25 NIV)

Commitment Two: Mid-Week Bible Study (Bible Prayer)

This is a commitment to attend weekly Bible study for the purpose of growing deeper in God and finding principles by which to live our lives. In this Bible study, we discover the promises of God and learn how to apply them to our lives. Attending Bible study helps us arrive at real maturity in the Lord and teaches us how to see things His way rather than our way. I learned that mature believers who have a firm understanding of God's Word are better prepared to go into the community and minister to people who have not accepted Christ or do not attend a church. Regular attendance at Bible study helps us get perspective. The Word of God encourages us with these words:

Let us stop going over the same old ground again and again, always teaching those first lessons about Christ. Let us go on instead to other things and become mature in our understanding, as strong Christians ought to be. Surely we don't need to speak further about the foolishness of trying to be saved by being good, or about the necessity of faith in God. (Heb. 6:1 TLB)

God wants us to give precedence to what is most important by keeping the main thing the main thing and not getting lost in elementary thoughts about the Christian life. It is for this reason Paul stresses the importance of studying the Word of God in this verse:

Study to shew thyself approved unto God, a workman that needeth not to be ashamed, rightly dividing the word of truth. (2 Tim. 2:15 KJV)

As you can see, it will take all of this and more to complete the vision God gave us for our ministry. Attending Sunday school (LDH) and Bible study faithfully speaks volumes to the commitment we need for His work.

Commitment Three: Serving in Ministry

This is a commitment for the members to serve in a ministry using their gifts, talents, and abilities to serve God and others at whatever the cost. In our small groups, one of our focus points is ministry. Our goal is to see every person in the group serving in a ministry of the church and participating in a community service project to get them outside of the church walls and into the community. Our church has ten small groups that are responsible for providing a service in the community at least four times a year. This gives us a total of forty community service projects a year. Our community service projects can be performed by caring for those who can't help themselves, singing Christmas carols, feeding the hungry, working with other community service agencies to aid them in their work, cutting grass for elderly people, painting homes in the community, and working with youth programs. There are countless opportunities for community service. Doing these things connects us with the Scripture that says,

Each one should use whatever gift he has received to serve others, faithfully administering God's grace in its various forms. (1 Peter 4:10 NIV)

It is God's grace that's making a difference in people's lives and in the community. No matter what things are like, when we properly administer the grace of God through our work in the community, it brings things back to order. For example, if we build one new home in a rundown neighborhood, there will soon be a change in the surrounding homes. The residents will start to show pride in their environment. When we show concern in our communities by applying our gifts to make a difference, we will soon see others doing the same. This is the kind of commitment it takes to make a community difference, and when people are using their gifts, it says they are ready for the task.

Commitment Four: Worshipping God with the Larger Body Weekly

This is a commitment to attend church weekly for worship and fellowship with the members of the body of Christ. This is a time for expressing our love to God in a corporate setting. We can't show our love for the community until we first show our love to God. Again, Jesus put it this way:

> "Love the Lord your God with all your heart and with all
> your soul and with all your mind." This is the first and
> greatest commandment. And the second is like it: "Love your
> neighbor as yourself." (Matt. 22:37–39 NIV)

Commitment Five: Paying Tithes and Offerings

This is a commitment to honor God with our finances. Giving Him what He asks of us is just as important as what He gives us. Tithing does more for the givers than they can see on their own. It brings blessings into people's lives and is supported by the Word of God.

"Bring the whole tithe into the storehouse, that there may be
food in my house. Test me in this," says the Lord Almighty,
"and see if I will not throw open the floodgates of heaven
and pour out so much blessing that you will not have room
enough for it." (Mal. 3:10NIV)

God promised He would bless us if we are obedient. Tithing
expresses our obedience and shows who is first in our lives. When
we give our tithes, we demonstrate that we love God more than we
love our money. Our tithing record can even be used as a tool to
perform a self-evaluation of our financial priorities. The Bible teaches
being God's way of establishing priority in our lives, as seen in this
Scripture:

The purpose of tithing is to teach you always to put God first
in your lives. (Deut. 14:23 TLB)

When God has precedence in our lives, we will be relieved of the
stresses we bring upon ourselves by being disobedient to Him. The
things we stress over are the things only God can provide, and when we
let Him have first place, we will see the difference. Jesus tells us what
to do in this verse:

But seek first his kingdom and his righteousness, and all these
things will be given to you as well. (Matt. 6:33 NIV)

There are a few needs that all humans have in common, such as
food, water, and clothing, and God promises to provide them if we put
Him first.

Therefore I tell you, do not worry about your life, what you
will eat or drink; or about your body, what you will wear.
Is not life more important than food, and the body more
important than clothes? Look at the birds of the air; they do
not sow or reap or store away in barns, and yet your heavenly
Father feeds them. Are you not much more valuable than
they? (Matt. 6:25–26 NIV)

Commitment Six: Winning Souls for Christ

This is a commitment to bring the lost and unconnected to Christ so
their lives will be changed. Everything we do in the church should be
related to winning souls for Christ, whether it is talking to people one
on one about Him or using our lives as examples so Christ can be seen
in us. The Great Commission of Jesus Christ states,

Therefore go and make disciples of all nations, baptizing
them in the name of the Father and of the Son and of the
Holy Spirit, and teaching them to obey everything I have
commanded you. And surely I am with you always, to the
very end of the age. (Matt. 28:19–20 NIV)

When the mission of the church reaches out and makes an impact
in the community, people are saved and lives are transformed. This is
why we as Christians need to always be ready to share the good news
of Jesus Christ. If we can effectively share the reason for the hope we
have in Christ, others may be convinced to put their hope in Him as
well. The Word of God encourages us to do so.

But in your hearts set apart Christ as Lord. Always be
prepared to give an answer to everyone who asks you to

give the reason for the hope that you have. But do this with gentleness and respect. (1 Peter 3:15 NIV)

The reason for the hope you have can be as simple as sharing why you love Jesus, study the Word, obey leadership, hold you position in your commitment, attend Sunday school and Bible study (Bible prayer), serve in ministry, worship God, pay tithes and offerings in your, church, or want to see people saved and going to heaven. When we give the reason for the hope we have, we are really sharing the benefits of our faith, and when people can see the benefits of our faith, it makes them want to honor God with their lives. The fact is, when we do the right things before people, the Scripture encourages us that men will give Him the praise.

Let your light shine before men, that they may see your good deeds and praise your Father in heaven. (Matt. 5:16 NIV)

When good deeds are shown in the community, it makes people praise God. When we share the resources God gives us, it connects people to a source greater than themselves, making a life-changing difference in their lives. God wants us to reach people and bring them into His presence.

"Well, then," said his master, "go out into the country lanes and out behind the hedges and urge anyone you find to come, so that the house will be full." (Luke 14:23 TLB)

With this newly reformed group, God was about to do something incredible to show the world and small churches that you don't have to be a mega-church to do great things for God. You don't have to be mega to take on challenges that will change your community and bring transformation into people's lives of people. Nevertheless, you do have to be committed. This small band of people who were still working on committing to the above nine areas of development proved to the city what God can do through people who trust Him.

Through this movement, God created one of the greatest community development movements that has ever been accomplished by a church within the city of Saginaw, Michigan. This movement is called Mission in the City, which we will talk about in chapter 10. My hope is that the work the Spirit has allowed us to accomplish will serve as a motivating factor or a proven model to increase the faith of leaders all over the world. It will show them their church is big enough to do everything Christ has for it to do, and through prayer, much more can be done. According to the Word of God,

Now glory be to God, who by his mighty power at work within us is able to do far more than we would ever dare to ask or even dream of—infinitely beyond our highest prayers, desires, thoughts, or hopes. (Eph. 3:20 TLB)

Chapter 10

Mission in the City

$\mathfrak{M}$ ission in the City (MITC) is a community-development organization given by God to do a specific work in the community and to produce a true and relevant need-meeting mission in the heart of the city. Mission in the City was given to assist in restoring the community back to good health through programs and services that give life to the people. The work of this mission is imperative for such a time as this because so much is missing in our cities. There are communities in need of restoration, and we can no longer depend on our local government to do the work alone; they can only do so much. I sensed the Spirit of God speaking to the church to produce community programs to help keep our city on the cutting edge. With all the churches in our communities, there is no reason why we can't lead the way in community development, reaching out to where the people are rather than waiting on them to come to us. Without effective, faith-based community programs coming from God, our cities will continue to decline.

My hope is that this chapter will be an inspiration to churches, community leaders, community organizations, leaders, and other initiatives to become more proactive in restoring and rebuilding their communities so cities around the world can again be safe and enjoyable places for people to live. With this in mind, I will share how Spirit of God shaped and used our church to create a community-development movement that's making a life-changing difference in our city. The focus will be in four areas: the history of Mission in the City, God's purpose for MITC, the scope of its services, and diverse partnerships.

The History

Mission in the City has an amazing history. The Lord's hand is seen throughout the development and function of the entire movement. As I stated in chapter 2, in 1999 God told me to lead the church to do a survey seeking the felt needs of the community, and following the survey, we entered our most painful time of ministry. This painful period lasted for about five years, from 2000 to 2005.

During this time, God's hand was upon me and inspired me to buy all the houses and land close to us. Being obedient to the direction of the Spirit, I began to inquire about the land one lot at a time, and we found favor with every property owner. Some of them gave us their lots, stating they "wanted the church to have them." Some sold their lots to us for as little as fifty dollars, others for five hundred, and several were in the thousands. However, none of them exceeded $12,000. By the end of 2005, we had purchased around fifty lots in our church community. God even blessed us to have enough adjacent lots to make an entire block, with the exception of a few houses people still occupy. Kirbyjon Caldwell helped me to somewhat understand the importance of land in his book *Entrepreneurial Faith*, where he says these encouraging words:

> Be careful how you manage the purchase and sell of your land
> for the purpose of maximizing your ministry. You need to
> look for ways to grow, not stay the way you are now.[8]

I can now plainly see how the Spirit was preparing us to change. When something is ordained by God to be, He will make things happen in advance to accompany the plan He has for us. He doesn't always tell us what He is doing, but things mostly turn out in our favor. I didn't know what God was preparing me and the church for, but I felt it could be something big. Without being inspired by Him, I would have never purchased any of the land. Coming out of the painful transition in 2006, the Spirit led us to make the needs we discovered in the community survey our Mission in the City. The land we bought was for the use of those highlighted needs.

With this in mind, I want to encourage all pastors to look out from where they are and establish a targeted area for community development in every direction of the church. The purchase of land can be used for expanding ministry one lot at a time, and over time you will have plenty of land to use for your vision programs. In our target area, we cover four blocks that go from north to south of the church and four blocks that go from east to west of the church. Our goal is to buy every piece of land in the target area that God makes available to us, large or small, even if the purchase doesn't make sense at the time. Land has always been of great value, even in Abraham's day.

---

8   Kirbyjon Caldwell and Walt Kallestad, with Paul Sorensen, *Entrepreneurial Faith*. (Colorado Springs, CO: Waterbrook Press, 2004), 21.

The Lord said to Abram after Lot had parted from him, "Lift up your eyes from where you are and look north and south, east and west. All the land that you see I will give to you and your offspring forever." (Gen. 13:14–15 NIV)

From this point, our mission work was fully established and declared to be our Mission in the City, serving as the 501 C-3 community-development arm of the church, with a purpose to

Make life better for people in the city of Saginaw and Saginaw County by improving and restoring the community one person, one block at a time.

The goal of MITC is to improve and restore our community through job creation, building recreational facilities, creating programs for adults and youth, feeding the hungry, changing lives, creating safe places for community gatherings, creating businesses, refurbishing and building new homes, and meeting other various community needs. With the help of God, these goals will become reality.

God's Purpose for Mission in the City

I believe the Lord ordained MITC for such a time as right now to help cities that are suffering from a plague of blight, violence, drug trafficking, unemployment, and gang activities. MITC will help change the environment and stabilize the community by restoring the missing parts that will make the community safe. When the environment changes, people will change, and when people change, there will be fewer life-threatening activities in the community.

I believe the Lord predestined Mission in the City to be a model for churches struggling to find ways to make a difference. This model shows them how to move beyond their walls and out into the community, making major investments through the implementation of programs and projects that will remove the negative reputation that afflicts their community. These investments will silence the cry of the world, which blatantly declares the church has nothing to offer the people who live in the communities that surround it. The critics who claim the church has never done anything of significance but build parking lots and new buildings to host their own private church parties and activities will be silenced. We have already witnessed significant change in our community and can serve as a witness of what God can and will do if people trust Him and step out on faith.

I also believe God ordained MITC to work with other community leaders and organizations to build a network of people to assist in promoting nonthreatening programs that make people want to continue their residence in the city. With the help of God and partnership with other community organizations, we can make dreams come true and revitalize the city. Again, Kirbyjon Caldwell says,

Entrepreneurial faith is not just about having a dream or receiving a vision from God. It is acting on the dreams and vision that God gives us.[9]

Those with entrepreneurial faith look beyond the walls of their surroundings and into the whole community.[10]

Reading these two quotes gave me the motivation to move forward. They inspired me to keep working hard toward the vision to restore our community. I learned vision isn't always easy, and the visionary must

---

9   Ibid., 12.

10   Ibid., 20.

be determined to press forward in spite of the obstacles that might appear if he/she plans to make a community difference. Our goal is not to just have a vision but to put the vision into action. Throughout the remainder of this chapter, I will detail the MITC programs, projects, and events as they relate to the scope of service the Lord God is using to reshape the church and the community. Before I elaborate on the scope of services, it would help to read a MITC recognition letter from the *city of Saginaw's mayor found in appendix VI.*

The Scope of Services

Programs, Projects, Events

The scope of service covers several programs, projects, and events that made MITC an icon in the city, and they can be used in every community with a guarantee to change the lives of the people. I will share the ones the Spirit gave us to restore our community in the order they took place; before I share them, I need to share how the work of the mission was affirmed at one of our Wolverine Baptist State Congress workshops. The study was from the book called *The External Focused Quest (Becoming the Best Church FOR the Community,* written by Eric Swanson and Rick Rusaw.

I took about fifteen people with me to glean information to help us improve our community work. At the end of the day, everyone was amazed to have discovered how community-driven our church already was. The focus of the workshop was on chapter 4, "They Lived in the Kingdom Story, Not a Church Story," and chapter 5, "The Few Send the Many, Not the Many Send the Few."[11] These two chapters provided the most life-changing information we could have read or discussed. At the

---

11   Eric Swanson and Rick Rusaw, *The Externally Focused Quest Becoming the Best Church FOR the Community.* (San Francisco, CA: Jossey-Bass, 2010), 70–89.

end of the workshop, we did a breakout session to discuss ten community-driven questions provided by the dean of Christian education in hopes of motivating us to return home and get busy with becoming the best church for the community. Our church answered all ten questions effectively and without any hesitation. The questions were as follows.

Question One: Based upon the presentation today, can people see the kingdom of God being realized through your church in your community?

Our Answer: Yes, they can! Our church is becoming known for programs we offer to the community.

Question Two: Based upon the presentation today, what actions can your church now take that reflect being kingdom-minded, according to Mathew 25:31–46, regarding the church doing things for Jesus by doing them for people in the community?

Our Answer: We are reaching out to the community by providing services to help them in many different ways, such as walking programs, a free health clinic, a recovery program, community recreation, and gardening.

Question Three: Externally focused churches record that giving and serving are the heartbeat of their churches. Based upon the presentation today, what adjustments must your church make to demonstrate the same action?

Our Answer: We built a first-class sports and fitness park that cost $250,000 for the people in our community, and we also have open a health clinic and a vegetable garden, along with many other community programs led by volunteers as part of our heart for the community.

Question Four: What changes could happen in your city if your church spent more time being busy for the kingdom outside its walls?

Our Answer: We have already affected change in our city by investing in restoring homes and buying empty lots to remove the blight from the community. If we continue to do this kind of work, it will bring about change in the lives of people, which will affect change in the community, causing people to want to continue living in our city. As ministers in our city catch this vision, we will work with them to show them how to improve their neighborhoods.

Question Five: Name some things your church does that directly benefit the community and not your church.

Our Answer: Our sports and fitness park is for the community, even if they belong to another church or don't have a church home, period. Our thinking is for people to know the church is concerned about them, as Christ is concerned. On a weekly basis, we give away clothes and home items for struggling families who don't attend our church.

Question Six: When Jesus left His marching orders to the early church, part of His commission included the scope of its mission. It was to make disciples in Jerusalem (the place where it was), Judaea (the country that contained Jerusalem), Samaria (the county to the north, populated by people the Jews historically despised), and to the ends of the world. Based upon the presentation today, how do you plan to reach people in your: A. Jerusalem (across the street), people who are like you who live, work, and play within your area? B. Judaea (across the community), people who are culturally similar to you but geographically distant? C. Samaria (across the track), people who are geographically close but culturally different? D. Ends of the earth—people who are culturally different and geographically distant?

Our Answer: A. By making sure the church has taken authority in the community by providing programs and events conducive to the entire neighborhood. B. By ensuring our programs and events are open to all people who are in need of our community services. C. By ensuring people of all backgrounds are welcome by personal invitation to share in the programs and events we have for the community. D. We will share our programs with the world by putting it in writing and on our website so people can have connection with our resources wherever they are in the world and to help them get started by availing ourselves to answer questions as needed.

Question Seven: Externally focused churches, by definition, are churches that believe the gospel is and has always been a message that is best expressed in words and works of love. Based upon today's presentation, what actions (in both areas highlighted) must your church take to demonstrate that it is becoming an externally focused church?

Our Answer: The work we are already doing is love in action. It makes us become doers of the Word of God. Out of love, we discovered what should be done for the people, and out of love, we give our time, talents, and resources to make it happen.

Question Eight: Externally focused churches have discovered that partnering with others is critical to becoming successful in missions.

Name a church (or churches) in your immediate community that is doing a successful, externally focused project that could benefit from your support (in terms of resources and physical commitment)?

Our Answer: I don't know personally any other church who has made it known to the community, but we are always looking to help others. I can only speak for our church in what we have done and how we could use the support and resources of others to help make things better. Our services are open to all in our community, whether they are churchgoers are not.

Question Nine: What externally focused project(s) is your church currently doing in your community that other churches/businesses have embraced and now support because the project is making a difference in other's lives?

Our Answer: We built a sport and fitness park that Lowe's Home Improvement and Citizens Bank helped us by investing their resources. We sponsor a health clinic that the Center of Hope organization helps us run. People from the community are now helping us run our programs.

Question Ten: Externally focused churches are effective because, over time, they have become globally and kingdom focused on a select few endeavors that are changing lives. Many churches, however, continue adding projects to a long list of things already in motion at the church that only spread resources (financial and human) thin and have little value and impact. What are some ways you can help your church become more focused on projects that build the kingdom?

Our Answer: Keep casting vision for the community you live in. Keep showing your congregation how they can change lives and even more lives if they keep making external investments that benefit the community because true love is an action that benefits others, even if they are not members of your church.

Before we move further, I encourage you to read another *MITC recognition letter written by our state representative in appendix VII.*

Programs

Twelve-Step Bible-Based Recovery

This program is an attempt to reach people in the community who have hurts, habits, and hang-ups destroying their lives. The goal is to bring them back into the community and help them overcome their addictions by replacing them with something more positive. Many of our recovery participants are now serving as leaders in the church and community. This program has reached over fifty community people who gather weekly for a time of sharing, learning, and encouragement.

I believe every church has people in its community who need help with addictions they can't overcome alone. Many of them feel no one cares. I prayed and asked God if He would send the people who feel unwanted to New Life. As a result of my prayer, God started releasing them weekly into our services and recovery program, and many of their lives were changed. I don't care what people say about the work of the church or its community programs; there are no substitutes for changed lives. We thank God for a recovery program that is working. People from all over the city are finding deliverance from different kinds of addictions, such as overeating, lying, smoking, or drinking. We celebrate with them as they recover and become restored back into the community. Some have been so successful that they have been appointed to be leaders in the church and in the recovery program to help others. The Spirit gave me the information to start this program at a study I did at a purpose-driven conference in Lake Forest, California.

Community Health Program

After putting things in place, God opened a door for us to partner with an agency called Center of Hope that works with Saint Mary's of Michigan, and together, we are making a difference. With their help, we provide a Family Life Health Clinic for the community. The purpose of the clinic is to meet the medical needs of the people. Services and referrals are free to those who need medical care and don't have insurance or are underinsured. The clinic is housed in one of the many houses we purchased and renovated and is open on the second Saturday of every month. It averages fifteen to twenty patients. This program speaks volumes to the community and gives hope to the hopeless.

Our goal is to help people have a better life. The services we offer are as follows, and any church can offer these services with the right connections:

- Free physical examinations (performed by volunteer physicians and nurse practitioners)
- Free blood pressure screenings
- Free blood glucose screenings
- Registered nurse services
- Referrals for vision services
- Referrals for prescription assistance
- Referrals for lab services
- Referrals for specialty services
- Referrals for mental health services
- Referrals for substance abuse services
- Free flu vaccinations (October, November, December)

- Health education/counseling
- Referrals for family doctor services

Our goal is to be a mission that is making dreams come true for others by providing the people with something they are having problems getting on their own.

Community Garden Program

The community garden is another part of our commitment to "restore our community one person, one block at a time." As part of a wide range of community support programs, MITC seeks to provide the members of the community with greater access to fresh fruits and vegetables, such as tomatoes, cucumbers, and much more.

In the first year of the garden, we provided food for over seventy-five families. Looking out and seeing people from the community sharing freely in the produce of the garden brought about such a great family feeling. We saw people who deeply appreciated the garden resources. This idea reminds me of when I was a young child living with my parents. When gardens were planted, everyone who lived in the community shared in the produce. All that was asked of the partakers was to not waste the produce, to take only what they needed, and to not damage the garden. There were many gardens where I came from, and everyone always had more than enough.

Our goal is to get the neighborhood involved so we can make the most of the gardening program. Our dream is for them to work with us by sponsoring a row in the garden, which they plant and cultivate. We will supply the tools, equipment, seeds, and water; all they have to do is pick the time they want to help in the garden. In doing so, we can develop a deeper appreciation for one another while protecting and caring for the crops and ultimately sharing the harvest with each other.

To have positive relationships in the community, programs and projects like these will make a world of difference.

Community Needs Program

This program is designed to help our community families by providing support and assistance with basic material needs. The program is designed to be part of a broad system of community-development programs that connect people to resources and gives them hope to lead a better life. Participation in the program is through referrals. We work with other collaborative partners who send people to us for this service. Our goal is to provide families with clothing, personal care items, and basic household items. We also use this program to help people who are getting out of prison to get a fresh start. We partner with stores like Home Depot and Bed, Bath, and Beyond and members of the church and other organizations.

This program is really giving hope to people who are struggling and seeking assistance. The word is out, and right now, we are receiving five to six calls a week asking for help and support. The program is structured so individuals first meet with the community needs director. Next the recipient has to fill out a request card and wait for an appointment to come in for assistance. We have other resource partners to pitch in if we can't help them, such as the United Way and other churches who work with us to make good things happen for people in need. We are always willing to work with anyone to make a positive difference in the community. We have assisted over 225 families with personal and household items within the last two years.

Sports and Fitness Park

After years of purchasing land in proximity to the church, God blessed us to own over fifty lots. In 2010, on a block of land adjacent to the church, we built a sports and fitness park to bring hope to the community. This park is one of many projects we are planning to build in the community to help restore it. It consists of a quarter-mile walking track, two full-size professional basketball courts, a pavilion equipped with electrical outlets, a commercial water fountain, and two barbecue slabs. For security purposes, the park is secured with a six-foot wrought iron fence and security lights. The park also has lots of grassy area for many activities and community programming opportunities. The sports and fitness park gives a facelift to the area by providing a positive attraction in the community.

In addition, the park serves as a hub for physical fitness and social activities in the neighborhood. Our hope is to assist in keeping the people in our church and community healthy by giving them a safe place to walk, run, and play. We believe through physical fitness, lives are prolonged. The pavilion provides a safe place for people to gather and celebrate special occasions like family reunions, picnics, birthday parties, and other social gatherings.

This undertaking was one of the biggest projects the church has ever embarked upon. It became the center of attraction throughout the city, and it was proudly reported by the people of the neighborhood and community leaders as one of the "biggest community projects ever done by a church." The park made history and will serve as a model for churches and organizations in restoring communities for years to come. As we unfold the programs and events that take place in the park, you will see that the work is life-changing and how the community supports the movement wholeheartedly.

The programs and events that have taken place in the park have made it one of the biggest community-connection pieces in the entire city. The work produces a feeling of completeness within that nothing else can do. Maybe it's because we are finally doing what God intended for the church to do all along, which is the development of the community.

As we approached the completion of the park, I began to visualize how much more could be done just by virtue of what had already taken place. Once you get started with community, you will be doing it for a very long time because the dream for it will just keep producing.

I am sharing this information because I believe every community has an area that needs to be developed, and many churches have an opportunity to own land through the land bank of their cities. The land bank can assist them with getting enough land to make something big happen and keep their communities vibrant and growing.

The Vision for the Sports and Fitness Park Funds

Before we got started, I met with the manager of our city a few times to discuss the project. I also made several trips to the city council meetings to share the vision for the park and to seek their permission to move forward. I learned through all of this how important it is to have the backing of the city when you are planning to do community work. They can make things much easier for you.

The total cost of the venture was a quarter of a million dollars. To get the money, I cast and recast the vision to build the park with many people, including banks, businesses, and organizations, to rally support from them. God showed us favor, and several of them gave dearly to help make the dream become a reality.

I will never forget the day when it was time to start building and we didn't have all of the money we needed. The members of the church and a few organizations had already given $175,000 to the project. The director of the project said to me, "What are we going to do?" We had told everyone the building of the park would take place at a certain time.

I had so much faith in God that I looked at the project director and said, "Tell the contractors I said start building."

He said, "How are we going to finance the work? We don't have all the money."

I told him, "It's not like they will complete the work by tomorrow."

In other words, by the time they finish the work, God will have given us everything we need, so start building. In the meantime, I was led to go see the team at Lowe's Home Improvement. They listened to my story as I shared my vision to improve our community by building this park and how the park would change lives in our community and give it a facelift that would attract many. They told me to apply for the Lowe's Community Grant. I did as instructed, and our story was so compelling that they gave us a $50,000 grant plus another $1,200 in store credits to help us.

Shortly after this, I went to see our banker, who we had been with since the beginning of New Life. I shared the vision with him, and he recommended I put in for a community grant. I followed his instructions, and before the park was complete, they gave us $25,000 to help with the project. In a matter of a few days, we were prepared to pay cash for the park and even had a few dollars left to do programming. If you are going to do community work for God, you must have faith with action and believe He will provide the resources.

Again, a movement of this magnitude must start with vision. The vision must be cast, and the people must catch it before it can become a reality. Vision shows people what needs to happen, why it needs to happen, and the outcome of it happening. A good illustration of these three statements can be found in Nehemiah's strategy to rebuild the walls of Jerusalem.

Then I said to them, "You see the trouble we are in: Jerusalem
lies in ruins, and its gates have been burned with fire. Come,
let us rebuild the wall of Jerusalem, and we will no longer
be in disgrace." I also told them about the gracious hand of

my God upon me and what the king had said to me. They replied, "Let us start rebuilding." So they began this good work. (Neh. 2:17–18 NIV)

Nehemiah showed them the problem, saying, "We are in trouble, and the city lies in ruin." People have to see the problem and admit its existence before they can get motivated to do something. Then he showed them what needed to happen and how they could help solve the problem by saying, "Come let us rebuild." Then he showed them the results of rebuilding by saying, "We will no longer be in disgrace." Then the people replied, "Let us start rebuilding." Rebuilding needs to occur if we are going to turn our communities around and make them flourish again.

Like Nehemiah, to build the park, I had to share with the people the condition of our city, noting that there was no recreation in the community. There was no safe place for adults to walk or to have community fellowship. Our city was lacking an outlet for the youth to communicate and build positive relationships that come from sports activities. We have seen firsthand how the lack of recreation can bring out the worst in the community.

I showed them how we could help fill the void by building a park and providing the space, equipment, and structure for it to happen. I also showed them the potential benefits of youth getting along through the creation of great relationships. The fact is, where there is no sound of recreational joy coming from the mouths of youth in the community, the community will die a slow death because there is nothing left for young people to do but get in trouble.

To really help them see the problem, I often painted a picture to show the difference between the west side of our city and the east side. The west side has everything a person could possibly need already in place, and the east side is suffering from a lack of basic needed resources. I made a point to talk about how crossing the bridge from the east side to the west side was like walking out of darkness into the marvelous light.

The west side is where people find recreation of every type—shopping centers, malls, movie theaters, restaurants, businesses, and beautiful houses and apartments. After enjoying the west side, returning to the east side was like walking out of the marvelous light back into the darkness where things are still the same; people are afraid to walk the streets because of gunfire, drugs, and other fearful activities. I made it clear to them that, with all of the churches on the east side of town, our city should not be in the shape it's in right now. Out of one hundred or more churches, if a little community work was being done by each of them, I can imagine the difference we would have made already.

After listening to all of this and catching the vision, they said, "Let's build," and we launched the Sports and Fitness Park Financial Campaign and raised over $250,000 to pay cash for the park within a single year. Building the park was proof that the people caught the vision.

> After Paul had seen the vision, we got ready at once to leave
> for Macedonia, concluding that God had called us to preach
> the gospel to them. (Acts 16:10 NIV)

When people catch the vision, they move quickly. A vision doesn't take ten years to do what God has inspired. They were convinced God had called them to do this work, so they moved with no hesitation or procrastination and made the vision become reality. This is exactly what it takes for every group, church, or organization to make something great happen in the community. Once the vision is cast, someone must catch it and move immediately, being totally convinced God has called them to do the work.

The Grand Opening of the Sports and Fitness Park

On June 11, 2011, we hosted the grand opening of the sports and fitness park. The opening day was phenomenal! Over two thousand people from the community and all over the city shared in this momentous event of dedication, celebration, and community appreciation.

The neighborhood residents had been waiting for so long to see something good happening around them. They felt that the church had finally made a difference in the community and that God had not forsaken our city. The celebration went on all day, and the community and the church fellowshipped together from 12:00 until 6:00 p.m.

A lady wrote me a note after the celebration that said, "I felt Saginaw was a wasteland, rather a desolate land. After seeing and experiencing your vision, this may be an incorrect view." I fully understood where she was coming from because the park brought a sense of hope through the joyful sounds of children and youth interacting and celebrating in a safe social environment that had been missing for three generations due to gunfire, drug trafficking, and gang activities. The activities have now been resurrected in the community through the activities of the park. Watching the youth as well as adults coming together is a guarantee for life in the community. Please read comments about the MITC Park written by a *former state recreation director in appendix VIII.*

At this event, we had the support of great people who believed in us and supported our work, such as our own city mayor and the mayor pro-tem, county commissioner, state representative, Wolverine Baptist State Congress president, pastors, and many more as speakers for the dedicatory service. The news media flooded the place and gave us great coverage on every television station, along with the Saginaw news reporters.

This event reminded me of the way things used to be in the city, forty years ago, when I first moved to Saginaw. Neighbors regularly came together and shared their lives. There were great community and family picnics in parks, and friends and neighbors played sports every weekend. In an effort to bring back the good ol' days, we provided entertainment from different gospel singing groups and instrumental music throughout the day. Some people participated in different kinds of exercise dances and others played sports, while the old timers sat under the pavilion, catching up on times past. Again I need to share the remarks that came from president of the Wolverine State Congress of Christian Education in *appendix IX.*

Summer Youth Camp

On June 13, 2011, following the grand opening of the park, we launched a nine-week community summer youth camp designed to teach character building and to assist parents in keeping their youth safe throughout the summer while they worked. This program averaged fifty-five children per day, Monday through Thursday, from 12:00 to 5:00 p.m. Any church or organization can implement this kind of program. In fact, programs like these are very important because children are often left unattended while school is out for the summer; this is the time most of them get in trouble. It is critical to get our community's youth involved in structured activities and programs with supervision to keep them safe.

We involved older leaders from the church family and community to help with our programs. We believe older people become energized while they are working with younger people. As they assist in leading recreational programs, it also benefits from them. The programs help them stay in shape and keep them young at heart. During our summer youth camp program, we focused on five things with the children to give them hope and bringing about change in their lives.

1. Food

Working with the Food Bank of Eastern Michigan, we provided a nutritious lunch and snacks to cover the five-hour period we shared with the children. Extra food was served by the SYC team as the day progress. During this time, we taught them discipline, good eating habits, table manners, and social fellowship while they ate.

2. Life Lessons

Following the meal, working with community organizations such as the Boy Scouts of America, Health Delivery, Underground Railroad, the fire department, and other leaders and professionals from the community, we taught life lessons daily, helping the youth make better choices for their lives. The focus for each lesson was on character building. We taught them how to conduct themselves in society and how to live respectable and responsible lives. We taught them about sexually transmitted infections and the harm they can cause if the guidelines and principles that come with sex are ignored. Please read the comments about this program from *Health Delivery, Inc., in appendix X.*

3. Purpose-Driven Recreation

During the five-hour period, we focused on developing their lives through recreation. The children rotated through four forty-five-minute sports sessions. Some they liked, and some they didn't. We never let a child sit out just because he/she didn't like a sport session. We did this to teach them that they can't always have it their way and there are times in life when they have to cooperate with others, even though the activity is not their favorite. Many of them wanted to play basketball only, but the way the program is designed, they have to go through all of the sports sessions. Again, the goal behind this approach was to teach discipline, not allowing them to do whatever they wanted but to place a sense of structure in their lives. As adults and young adult leaders, we modeled positive social interactions, which enhances communication and sets the stage for teaching them how to get along and enjoy each other without fighting. We taught them the power of teamwork in sports by helping them see that one person can't win a game alone, but with the help of others, much can be accomplished.

4. Back-to-School Parent and Child Funfest

The closing of the nine-week summer youth program was incredible. The entire seventy-five-member staff, including the lunch servers, community leaders, security, and serve team members, participated to give the program a good closing. We brought the parents in to share in parent-and-child activities and a fellowship meal, and then we provided every youth with back-to-school supplies. The youth were excited and sad as they closed out the last day of the program. The last things they did for the evening was perform an encouraging dance touching the heart of their parents to the song called, "I Smile," by Kirk Franklin. Over three hundred people attended this grand event.

5. Youth Mentorship

Our teams didn't just work with the youth; they worked for change of conduct. The goal was not to provide a babysitting service. We used the older youth, ages sixteen to eighteen, to help teach the younger group. Our goal was to make them more responsible by giving them responsibility so we could teach them accountability. Working along with the adult leaders, they learned how to become responsible.

On some days, the staff gave each older youth a smaller child to mentor through the course of the day. They taught them how to do things, like tying their shoes or something they might have a problem doing. This helped build and strengthen relationships. We expected the young people to have physical run-ins at times and want to fight. If they did, we simply brought them together and spoke to them about the purpose of the program and helped them to apologize, hug, and make up, or they would have to leave the park and would have to return with their parents to continue. As you can see, it was engrained into the entire youth summer camp program.

Mentoring is a powerful tool to help shape the mind-set of young people, regardless of the size of your program, according to some information I got from www.beamentor.org. To read the information, *please see appendix XI.*

First Community Picnic

We hosted our first community picnic on July 30, 2011. At this gathering, we provided food, entertainment, and an opportunity for wholesome community conversations. People came from every direction to share in this fellowship. A safe place for an outdoor community gathering had been missing for so long, and people were amazingly grateful to be a part of the event. To really enhance this event and to make it more memorable, we provided household items for the needy in the community.

To make the picnic a success, all of our shepherd and purpose leaders came together to organize the food and activities for the entire event. Motivating the rest of the church to get involved, together, we were able to make a visible statement that showed the residents our community was not dead but was being rejuvenated through community fellowships, sports, and sharing in wholesome conversation. Over four hundred people shared in this life-changing fellowship event and left with great anticipation of the next gathering.

Purpose-Driven Community Basketball

The community youth waited patiently for the completion of the park. I watched many of them bounce basketballs on the sidewalks and while walking down the streets in great anticipation of playing ball soon. Shortly after the park was open, the sound of recreation was flowing back into the community. Our goal was to get some form of organized recreation going as soon as possible so we would have a way of keeping the programs safe and healthy. Being purpose-driven means they play with purpose. On some days they have open basketball, and others days they are playing team basketball; sometimes it's the challenge of other sports, like football or volleyball.

Purpose helps control large crowds, and without it, things can easily get out of hand. The very first year of opening the park, we averaged 247 participants weekly. I believe much of this can be credited to people feeling free because we had made it safe. For the entire summer, we had no fights among the youth participants. They were actually overprotective of the park because it had given them hope of building relationships and having something positive to do. We also challenged the older young adults to care for the park by keeping it clean and working with us in some of our other youth programs as a way of giving back. Our community basketball program is designed to help build good health and long-lasting relationships.

I never will forget when one of our local professional basketball players held a rally for the youth at Saginaw Valley State University called, "Man Up." A question was asked to this effect: "What makes you guys so angry?" and "How can you control your anger?" A young man about seventeen years of age, from whom I was sitting across, said, "If we had a safe place to play basketball and some people to work with us, we wouldn't be angry. We are angry because people act like they don't care about us." I knew then the dream to build a sports and fitness park and to have programs like this was ordered by God.

Three-on-Three Basketball HoopFest

Our first annual three-on-three Basketball HoopFest event was held on September 24, 2011, on the new basketball courts. We wanted to attract as many young people as possible to this event. We knew that through them, life would once again take its place in the community. This event was amazingly great! Over four hundred people attended. This hoopfest helped us in two distinct ways.

1. It served as a mission to connect with the youth in our community.

To do this, we rallied as many sponsors as possible to underwrite the expenses for each of the three- to four-person teams. Our hope was for some of the youth to gain a deeper appreciation for adults after experiencing the blessings of God through people's sacrifice and generosity. The adults gave them something they loved, and it was free. Styled as a three-on-three elimination tournament, church members and community leaders sponsored thirty-one teams. This program also served to get more adults involved in working with the youth in our community. This tournament made a way for the community's youth and adults to spend the entire day together.

The group with the largest participation in the HoopFest was the youth between the ages of thirteen and eighteen. We reached out to this age group because they participated in community basketball at the park on the weekly basis. The park security workers and others talked to these players about signing up for the tournament. We communicated with them as we saw them playing ball in the street as well. They were all excited about the event and signed up to play. All the youth worked with us in keeping the event safe. We gave out first-, second-, and third-place trophies and T-shirts to all players. This type of community activity has been missing for many years. I remember when we used to have the Gus Macker Basketball Tournament in the '80s. It was so much fun. We even had several teams from our church playing every year. This event has been gone for years, and we are hoping our HoopFest will at least bring back some of those good days.

2. It served as a tool to reveal the mindset of the youth in the community.

For some reason, the age group of nineteen and up did not participate in the HoopFest. I believe they just didn't see the value of having positive recreation back in the community since there had been three generations of people who had missed out on it. We couldn't inspire them to play, even though it was free. This age group played community basketball, but when it came to the tournament, none of them signed up. Seeing this age group not participating gave me more motivation to push even harder for the next tournament because the mind-set of this group must change. This incident really helped me understand our mission even more (to restore our community one person one block at a time). Plus I learned that good community basketball produces certain benefits in the lives of those who participate, according to Factoidz website. *Please see appendix XII.*

Steps for Health Community Walking Program

Since the opening of the park in June of 2011, we have provided a place for the community to walk to maintain their health. To date, we have averaged 187 adult walkers weekly. People come all times of the day to use the quarter-mile walking track. We want people to prosper in their health as they prosper in every other area of human development.

The walking track is the most amazing program we offer the community and its residents. The track was built with an asphalt substance providing a little cushion as people walk. The walking track is six feet wide, allowing two people to walk together side by side, sharing in great conversation together. The walkers are entertained by other activities as they walk, which keep them focused, even if they are walking along. They also feel free and secure as they walk because there is security all day long. In the future, our goal is to provide every walker with pedometers and awards for completing the walking program. I discovered there are also great benefits that come with walking, according to the Mayo Clinic at www.mayoclinic.com. *Please see appendix XIII.*

Sports and Fitness Park Rules

To execute change and to bring stability back into our community, we developed a set of rules to protect the people and the park, which all participants must follow to participate. The rules are made up from the very things people are used to doing and shouldn't be doing.

We were challenged with a few of the rules during the first week the park was open. The rule against duffel bags was one of our main challenges. One young man tried to bring a bag into the park, but when we asked him to check his bag, he immediately turned around at the gate. If he was clean, he should have let the security check his duffel bag.

We faced another challenge when a member of the community blatantly refused to comply with a serve team leader by telling him what he was not going to do regarding the program because he felt he was too old for the leader to be telling him what to do. We experienced two or three who wanted to fight and caught one putting a little brother over the fence. One young man came with sagging pants. He was asked to leave and not return in that fashion, and he never returned.

Some people have become so comfortable doing their own thing that they refuse to take part in a social outlet with rules. Some came to see if they could fit in and decided not to return. Some came to see if our rules would be enforced, and when they realized we were serious about them, they decided not to return because they were not used to structured programs. We were not alarmed about any of this because we knew the community's conditions before we started. We prayed that our program would change the way the young people think. The ones who embraced the idea of community bought into the program with their hearts and are now helping us truly make a life-changing difference. To see the rules for the park, please see *appendix XIV.*

Where there is no vision, the people perish. (Prov. 29:18 KJV)

Now to him who is able to do immeasurably more than all we ask or imagine, according to his power that is at work within us. (Eph. 3:20 NIV)

Please read our last recognition letter about our community work from our city hall *director of development in appendix XV.*

Chapter 11

Community Partnerships

How to Get Others Involved in Your Community Work

In this chapter, I will share to some extent how to get people to use their resources to help you perform community work. Eric Swanson and Rick Rusaw, the authors of the book, *Externally Focused Quest, Becoming the Best Church FOR the Community,* said two powerful things about partnership.

> Partnering and collaboration are not essential for becoming the best church in the community but absolutely essential if you want to be the best church for the community.[12]

---

12 Ibid., 111.

Churches that are transforming communities don't divide over their differences but unite with others churches and community organizations (faith based or not) around their common love for the community. We can unite and work together with other churches and other groups in our communities not because we share the same theology but because we care about the same things.[13]

I found out through the work God has allowed our mission to do that there are people and organizations outside of the church who will invest in ideas if they are compelling, fulfilling, and need meeting. Having community partners will help you do more than you can do alone. Many times we want to do something great for the community, but we don't have the money to make it happen or are not able to articulate our ideas to those who can help us. If we are going to make an impact with the church, we must find people, organizations, and businesses who will invest into our plans to make our community better. I have learned that we can do so much more working together.

Before I show you the power of partnerships in this chapter, I must share an important piece of information God revealed to me at a conference, which will set you up for real partnerships. I have labeled this information as the four necessities for a life-changing community program that will attract resources for your community organization.

When I was enrolled in the leadership training program at the Beeson Institutes with Dr. Dale Galloway, one of our sessions was held at the Purpose-Driven Church in Lake Forest California, in 2006. I had the privilege to hear Dr. Rick Warren's lecture on purpose. He shared with us four effective tools I called the four P-words, and I have been using them in all of my planning since I attended the leadership

---

13 Ibid., 114.

training: purpose, program, people, and place. He stated if we can answer these four words, our work will be successful, and if any of them are missing, our program will suffer tremendously.

When I look back over the years, I can see how this information would have helped me greatly to put things in place to grow a great ministry for God and the church. Though I didn't have the information back then, I have it now and can testify the information is true and powerful. I encourage every leader who is seeking direction to use this information.

I want to put this teaching in my own words and share my thoughts through my interpretation and application of the teachings. I learned that when building partnerships, these four words are essential, and answering each of them will be the determining factor in receiving help from partners.

The First P Is for Purpose

There must be a purpose for every area of your community ministry, large or small, to give direction to your destination. Purpose speaks to your vision—where you are going with your organization. It paints a picture showing you what it looks like at the end of your destination. A clear purpose describes what you see. It's a mental picture that gives you the energy and passion to make what you see happen when you look at it. To attract partners, you must be able to define your purpose/vision with as few words as possible. It must be written so people can read and follow it, as seen in these two verses:

And the Lord answered me, and said, Write the vision, and make it plain upon tables, that he may run that readeth it. (Hab. 2:2 KJV)

After Paul had seen the vision, we got ready at once to leave for Macedonia, concluding that God had called us to preach the gospel to them. (Acts 16:10 NIV)

The purpose/vision has to be clear enough to be written down, brief enough to be remembered, and specific enough to be achieved. As with Paul, Luke said after Paul had seen the vision, they got ready at once to leave, concluding that God had called them to do the work. Good vision will produce this kind of reaction in the lives of people.

The Second P Is for Programs

Good programs are the legs to getting the vision to its destination. The programs become your mission, which speaks to how you're going to make the vision happen. The programs you put in place will determine if your vision will become a reality. If you can't see how your programs will make the vision a reality, you should not use them. If they are not working, then you must seek God's direction to change them. Once the purpose is in place, you will be able to determine the programs you should be using, which will also help you evaluate and measure the success of the organization.

Our ministry has changed tremendously since God gave me this information. Every program we use now matches the vision. It hasn't always been this way for us. I really believe it was because I was determined to find my place with God that He made this information available to me, and now He is making it available to the readers of this chapter who may not have known. Again, if your programs are not working, don't be afraid to change them. Remember, God honors plans that are left to Him for the final word.

We should make plans—counting on God to direct us. (Prov. 16:9 TLB)

The Third P Is for People

Every program should only be launched after leadership and workers are chosen and given enough training to run them effectively. Sometimes this is the hardest one to put in place. People push the mission, and the mission pushes the vision. Therefore, great visionary thinkers and workers are imperative because they will keep the vision moving forward. If the people can't see where you are going (vision), they will never understand the significance of running the programs (mission), effectively. Most leaders can answer some of these questions; they believe they know where they are going, they have programs in place, but they may not necessarily be vision connected. No matter what programs are used, it is essential that qualified people are enlisted to carry them out, or the vision will not become reality.

Connecting the right people to the right program is critical because programs plus the right people get good results. People don't have to be members of your church to help you with community programs, but they do need direction to follow and accountability. Some of your greatest gifts are somewhere in the community and are not being used, and you must find a way to connect and get them involved without pressuring them to go to church. Transformation comes through personal involvement. Our hope is that one day they will start attending church on their own.

Our goal is to empower people throughout the community to help run our community programs by building partnerships with individuals who are willing to invest their time, talents, and gifts to make a difference in our community. With this in mind, we are constantly talking to people about investing and reinvesting into our community work by committing to work for a certain period of time. Remember, everyone is good at something.

Why is it that he gives us these special abilities to do certain things best? (Eph. 4:12 TB)

The Fourth P Is for Place

For every program you start, you must have a place to run the program. It doesn't matter how big the dream; if you don't have a place to carry it out, it's no good. As we think about purpose, programming, and people, it is essential that we think about place. Understanding the above information will help you develop partners in your city who will help you make things happen by using their resources, if you can provide them with a compelling purpose, programs, competent people, and a place to do it. From this point, I will shift the focus to the power of building partnerships.

Building Partnerships

Our community programs opened up so many doors to connect with people and get them involved in the community work. Our first annual summer youth camp employed over seventy-five volunteers on a rotating system to work with our youth. We used our security team and our serve team volunteers to change the lives of the youth enrolled in the camp. These park volunteers are from the church and the community and have been cleared by the Department of Human Services. The community basketball program provides great opportunities for several people to serve as well. The walking program calls for people to get involved. When it comes to building community, many people need to work together to make things happen. The community has different needs; therefore, we have different kinds of partners to help us meet those needs. With this in mind, we reached out to build a community network of partners consisting of the following.

I. Community Partners

• Community Residents

We reached out to the residents of our community to support the programs and to assist in helping us keep our youth motivated as we provide service to them. There are many talented people in every community who would love to help if your programs are compelling. Some of the people who helped us were members of other churches and lived on the other side of town, but they loved what we were doing and signed up to help. They worked in teaching, recreation, or security to help us make a difference.

• Teachers/Community Leaders

We also enlisted schoolteachers within our community to help us conduct our life lessons classes and to assist wherever they could. Our goal was to keep the youth's minds active and engaged during the summer so they wouldn't lose connection with what they had already learned during the school year.

• Coaches

We asked coaches from all over the city to join forces with us during the summer break and use their talents to teach the fundamentals of basketball, soccer, golf, softball, and track. We purposely focused on some sports our youth were not very familiar with just to introduce them to another sport they might like. These are just a few ideas we explored for our program.

II. Community Organization Partners

We reached out to community organizations to help us build character within the youth. We brought in people from the following organizations to help:

- Boy Scouts of America
- Girl Scouts
- Underground Railroad
- Health Delivery
- Saginaw Fire Department Administration

We sat down with each of them to discuss ways they could help us make a difference in the lives of our youth. I cast the vision of where we were headed, and they gave us feedback on how they could help. We implemented many of their ideas into our program, and the programs have been a great success.

III.   Community Collaborative Partners

To make great things happen in a community, there are certain organizations you must have on your team. They can either give you information or help make things become reality. The following organizations helped us tremendously:

- Saginaw Alignment Collaborative
- Great Start Collaborative
- Saginaw City Hall
- Saginaw City Council
- Saginaw County Commissioners
- United Way
- Center of Hope
- Department of Human Services
- Parishioners on Patrol

We also partnered with our local law enforcement to work with us in patrolling the community to ensure the safety and security of those utilizing the park. People quickly took note when they saw the Michigan State Troopers, Saginaw City Police, and the Saginaw County Sheriff's Department making their presence known by routinely driving through the neighborhood or stopping by for a few minutes. Needless to say, their presence spoke volumes to anyone who might have thought about causing trouble.

IV.   Financial and Resource Partnerships

The idea for building financial partnerships was to finance our community programs through people who would invest their resources in our work. In preparation for communicating this idea to others, I read a book called *Not Your Parents' Offering Plate* by J. Clif Christopher, who provided immeasurable insight on how to get people to give to your mission. These ideas were used in developing our financial partners, which I will discuss later. There are several things he taught me that helped us build strong partnerships with donors who gave to support the vision. I want to share a few quotes.

In chapter 2, he stated three reasons for why people give to your vision. I will only give the reasons, not the details. I highly suggest you read the book for yourself and glean the nuggets he dropped. *The first reason he said people give* is when there is "a belief in the mission"; the *second reason people give* is when they have "regard for staff leadership"; and *the third reason people give* is when they can "trust the fiscal stability of the institution."[14]

This book is a must read book for any leader who is planning to do community work. The teachings of this book will show you how to get doors to open for you and set you at the table with millionaires who

---

14   J. Clif Christopher, *Not Your Parents' Offering Plate.*

(Nashville, TN: Abingdon Press, 2008), 13, 21, 28.

are looking for programs and organizations in which to invest their resources. Just as the Scripture says in Proverbs,

A man's gift maketh room for him, and bringeth him before great men. (Prov. 18:16 KJV)

In planning our community work, I used this information and was helped tremendously in connecting with the funds/resources to help finance the work. At this point, I want to share with you the organizations/institutes I had the pleasure of sharing our vision with and how they responded to my request.

The First Partnership: New Life Baptist Church Family

I cast vision to the members of our church about the community development's sports and fitness park and explained to them how the park would effect change into our community. I asked as many as could to give $5,000 and the others to give what they could, and along with some community people, they gave $175,000 in eight months. This reminded me so much of our first building fund project in 1986. The people responded immensely.

The Second Partnership: Lowe's Home Improvement

One day as I was thinking and praying about who else we could call on for financial help, and the Lord placed Lowe's Home Improvement store on my mind. A couple of people from our organization and I made an appointment with them, and I shared our community-development dream with the store managers. They bought into the vision and gave in a big way to support our mission. This was the biggest grant ever given by their company. Our program was competing for funds with a program in another state, but ours was found to be the most compelling and convincing project for them to invest their money. In February 2012, we presented the Lowe's Home Improvement store with a picture of the sports and fitness park they helped us build, and the picture is hanging in their store for everyone to see.

The Third Partnership: Citizens Bank

As I continued to seek places to make my financial request, I was led to the bank where we had done business for our entire twenty-six years as a church. I spoke with our banker and shared with him our dream, and he recommended we apply for a community-development grant. Shortly afterward, we applied and were not successful. Through our faith to not give up, they called us to come in and meet with the board. I shared with them our community dream and how our dream would make a difference in the community. I told them how the project would change lives in our community and bring about a degree of stability in making people want to live in our city. After hearing and feeling our heart to help our community, they gave in a big way to help with the project. We know only God can work miracles like these, and only people of passion can understand the needs of the community. In February 2012, we also presented Citizens Bank with a picture of the sports and fitness park they helped us build.

The Fourth Partnership: Frankenmuth Jaycees

The director of our community-development mission spoke with a group called the Frankenmuth Jaycees, and after hearing what our mission was about, they gave handsomely to the project. They were happy to help us, and when they heard our vision, they responded quickly, with no hesitation.

The Fifth Partnership: Saginaw City Hall

I felt led to call upon our city to support us in our efforts to make a community difference. I shared first with the city manager the vision for our mission, and he thought our plans were compelling. He also felt our dream would be a great asset to help keep money coming into our city and the program at large would be a good model for the state of Michigan to combat crime and to restore community values. From there, I met with the city council and shared with them the dream and asked them to make us part of the city's block grant program. Even now, the gracious hand of God has allowed the city of Saginaw to help buy recreation equipment, put in professional basketball courts, and support other programs needed to run our summer youth camp. God has blessed Mission in the City to qualify, and the city has been a great help in working and believing in our mission.

The Sixth Partnership: Bed, Bath, and Beyond

This local store provides our community-needs program with items to help meet the needs of many community people. They share with us pillows, comforter sets, blankets, sheets, towels, curtains, rugs, cookware, trash cans, outdoor mats, and many other household items. Many people have benefited from this program, all because there are companies like these who are willing to help.

The Seventh Partnership: Home Depot

This local store provides our community-needs program with many different building and home repair items the community can use to improve the quality of living. We give the items to the community as people have need for them. We also hold special days where we put the items out so people can pick out what they need. There are so many ways for people to help if the vision is compelling. Home Depot did not give money; they gave merchandise to help support the vision and our community-needs program.

The Eighth Partnership: Loon's Baseball Foundation

We spoke with the representatives of the Loon's Baseball Foundation about our vision for the park. We shared with them our desire to keep our youth occupied during the summer to keep them out of trouble. They became one of our partners and gave us a grant to help meet the needs of our summer program.

The Ninth Partnership: Saginaw Community Foundation

After speaking with a representative of the Saginaw Community Foundation, I showed her pictures of what we were already doing in the community and shared how our programs were impacting the lives of the youth. In addition, I asked if the foundation could help us financially. We were approved for a grant, and we used the funds to help us purchase more sports equipment and to support other program activities.

The Tenth Partnership: Molina's Health Care

This group heard about our mission and gave us a Community Champion Award for the work we do and partnered with us in developing community gardening. They provided financial resources to help purchase gardening equipment.

Because we *asked* these organizations and institutions, we were able to build a sports and fitness park that cost $250,000, and we paid cash for the work and money for the installation of recreation equipment, which amounted to over $300,000. We are a living witness of what organizations and agencies will help you do if you can show them what you bring to the table. I highly encourage everyone who is thinking about community in this way to read J. Clif Christopher's book *Not Your Parents' Offering Plate.* Read it and ask God to show you how and who you can ask to help you.

> Two are better than one, because they have a good return for
> their work: If one falls down, his friend can help him up. But
> pity the man who falls and has no one to help him up! Also,
> if two lie down together, they will keep warm. But how can
> one keep warm alone? Though one may be overpowered, two
> can defend themselves. A cord of three strands is not quickly
> broken. (Eccles. 4:9–12 NIV)

Conclusion

To the best of my ability, in an effort to be a blessing to leaders and organizations, I have shared my life story as a pastor. I shared how the blessings of God were upon our ministry during its embryonic period, causing it to prosper in every sense of the word. Following that success, I experienced the most painful time in the ministry when it figuratively died due to changes being made too soon and a lack of vision. Out of the pain, God birthed a vision for the church that had been missing for some years and shaped me to become a visionary leader.

In this book, I explained the function of the vision and mission with emphasis on the expected outcome when they work together as God designed them. I identified the vision pillars, which are also the top four core values of the church—intellectual, physical, spiritual, and social development—and created a chapter for each of them to show how together they provide the balance we need in our everyday lives, along with programs that assisted in the development of each of them. I exposed a new idea for ministry called shepherding, which consists of people with a shepherd's heart working together to put the vision into action by nurturing and caring for age-appropriate groups in the development of the vision pillars.

I shared how the Spirit of God worked with me to rally the parishioners to help the church move from building parking lots to building community, with emphasis on a community-development program designed to restore the community one person, one block at a time and to bring life to a dying city. This community-development program allowed us to provide hope to adults and children, which has changed lives and brought stability to the community.

I provided invaluable information on how to rally support from organizations and people who will help make dreams something tangible by using their resources to support qualified organizations if the vision is compelling.

I really felt a need to write this book because people need to hear more stories that will renew their faith as they pray to make changes in their churches and communities. There are so many leaders who know they need to do something but are afraid to move against their fears. I believe the testimony and stories in *From Death to Life* will help them see what God can do once they take a step of faith.

I know this information will be of great significance to many. It remains a fact that pastors must make changes to keep the church relevant and current or they will risk losing out, whether they want to or not. This information is critically important for small church leaders, inspiring them to know they don't have to be big to do big things for God. However, they do need faith to move against their fears.

In retrospect, I can see the hand of God moving. He had a plan for New Life Church to be one of His model churches for ministry today—a time when ministry will make the most difference. The whole process reminds me of the Scripture that says,

"For I know the plans I have for you," declares the Lord,
"plans to prosper you and not to harm you, plans to give you
hope and a future." (Jer. 29:11 NIV)

It is mainly my hope that this book will impact the lives of pastors
in a compelling way by giving them new hope or renewed faith that will
motivate them to step out of their comfort zones and let God use them to
be model churches in their own communities by doing things they have
never done, going places they have never gone, attempting things much
bigger than themselves, and taking risks so they too can experience the
majesty and awesomeness of God's power in their ministry.

Based on my personal experiences with God in becoming a visionary
leader, I want to give encouragement to every reader of this book. If you
have to go through something to get to where God wants you to be,
it is only a process to prepare you for the task ahead so you can do the
work effectively, as seen in Scripture.

Consider it pure joy, my brothers, whenever you face trials of
many kinds, because you know that the testing of your faith
develops perseverance. Perseverance must finish its work so
that you may be mature and complete, not lacking anything.
(James 1:3–4 NIV)

About the Author

Pastor Rufus Bradley Sr. was born in 1952 in Arkansas and has been married to Relinda Bradley for thirty-seven years. They have two children, June and Rufus Jr., and four grandchildren.

Educational Background

Pastor Bradley is a graduate of United Bible Institute of Flint, Michigan, an extension of United Theological Seminary in (Monroe, Louisiana), where he earned a bachelor's degree in religious education. He has also completed the Advanced Leadership Training Program provided by the Beeson Institute, a program of Asbury Theological Seminary, where he traveled to nine states and worked with nine different mega-church leadership teams to enhance his skills in the areas of visionary leadership, mentoring, and theoretical and practical knowledge.

Community Leadership Involvement

Pastor Bradley is the founding pastor of New Life Baptist Church, where he has served for twenty-seven years, and is the founder of Mission in the City, a community-development organization that has existed for six years. He is an instructor and workshop facilitator for the Wolverine State Baptist Congress of Christian Education. He has served on the Vision Casting Team for the Lutheran Association of Saginaw, Michigan, and as a member of Alignment Saginaw, a leadership group created to improve quality of life by promoting collaboration among businesses, agencies, and institutions in Saginaw County. He is also a member of the Community Affairs Committee of Saginaw, Michigan.

Pastor Bradley also received an honorary doctorate of divinity from the Union Baptist Seminary, Inc., in Birmingham, Alabama, in July of 2012 for his insight and commitment to the rehabilitation and sustainability of the community.

Awards

Under his leadership, New Life Baptist Church and Mission in the City have received numerous recognitions and awards from the state of Michigan, the city of Saginaw, the Saginaw County Board of Commissioners, and other local political bodies for their work in the community. Some of these awards are: the key to the city, Zeta Amicae (the Auxiliary of Saginaw), Community Service Award, the Dr. Martin Luther King Jr. Community Service Award, the Molina Health Care Community Champion Award, the A. Phillip Randolph Community Service Award, the Restoration Community Outreach Service Award, the Wolverine Baptist State Congress Community Service Award, and the CAC Partners against Poverty Award.

For more information please contact:
Pastor Rufus Bradley
1401 Janes Ave.
Saginaw, MI 48601
(989) 753-1151

Appendix J

FIRST SALEM
MISSIONARY BAPTIST CHURCH

Pastor
Rev. Craig Tatum

Mission:

Reconciliation

of All Mankind

to Jesus Christ

II Corinthians 5:16

Vision:

Transforming

lives through

the preaching,

witness

and teaching

of God's

Holy Word.

Act 2:41-47

March 7, 2012

Rev Dr. Rufus Bradley, Sr., Pastor
New Life Ministries
1401 Janes Avenue
Saginaw, MI 48601

Beloved Dr. Bradley:

It is my distinguished honor to provide my assessment of the class you provided instruction for the Congress entitled "Biblical Application through Scripture Memorization."

First of all, we were looking for a class that would stimulate believers to develop a hunger for memorizing the Word of God.

Secondly, we were looking for a class that would provide a methodical approach to understanding basic principles and precepts of the bible.

Thirdly, we were looking for a class that encouraged student confidence based upon the tools they were equipped with as a result of the class.

Finally, we were looking for an instructor astute enough to articulate our needs in such a way that students would receive the instruction and leave more empowered to become impactful in their churches. The class, "Biblical Application through Scripture Memorization," and you, the instructor, were highly successful in meeting our needs without reservation.

With every class, we generally gain feedback from participating students through evaluation. Your class echoed: How grateful students were for the class; how they now have a more effective way of studying/memorizing the bible, how they appreciated your wisdom, wit and enthusiasm, not to mention your ability to articulate the memorization tools in such a simplistic way that it made learning easier, swift and effective.

Because of the success of this class, we are poised to offer the class again this year, expecting the same results. I would highly recommend this class to anyone struggling to memorize God's Word. I assure you, based upon the outcome of our Congress session, they will achieve success in memorizing the bible based upon your instruction and methods.

Serving the King,

Rev. Dr. Craig A. Tatum, Dean
Wolverine State Congress of Christian Education

251

Appendix JJ

The Benefits of Aerobics

- Lowers high blood pressure.
- Increases the high-density lipoprotein (HDL) in the blood, which helps collect cholesterol in the blood and dispose of it in the liver.
- Lowers the plasma triglyceride levels (fatty substances).
- Assists in weight control, mainly by reducing body fat.
- Improves the function of the heart by promoting beneficial changes in the structure and function of the coronary arteries (which provide oxygen to the heart muscle).
- Alleviates muscle pain and improving walking capability in people who suffer from peripheral arterial disease.[15]

---

15   Universal Fitness Tester, www.aerobictest.com, accessed February 17, 2013.

NAME	PHONE	6-Jan	MW	13-Jan	MW	20-Jan	MW	27-Jan	MW
Ann		P	A/P	P	P	P	P	P	P
Debbie		P	P	P	P	P	P	P	P
Susan		P	P	A/S	P	A/S	A/S	A/S	P
Marie		P	A/P	P	P	A	P	P	P
Linda		A	A	P	P	A	A/S	P	P
Gladys		P	A	P	P	P	P	P	P
Evette		P	A/P	A	P	A	P	A	P
Tony		P	A	P	A/P	P	P	P	A/P
Michael		P	A	P	A/P	P	P	P	A/P
David		A	P	P	P	P	P	P	P
Willie		P	P	P	P	P	A/S	P	P
James		P	A/P	P	P	P	P	P	P
Alex		P	P	P	P	P	A/S	P	P
Robert		P	P	P	P	P	P	P	P
Charles		P	A/P	P	P	P	P	P	P
Dorothy		A/S	A/P	A/S	A/P	A/S	P	A/S	A/P
George		P	P	P	P	P	P	P	P
Jimmy		P	P	P	P	P	P	P	P
Tina		P	P	P	P	P	P	P	P
Sally		P	P	P	P	P	P	P	P
Tom		A/S	A/S	A/S	A	A	A/S	A/S	A
Steve		P	A	A	A	P	P	A	A
Barbara		A/S	A/S	A/S	A/S	A/S	A/S	A/S	A/S
Marcus		A	A/P	A/P	A/P	A	A/S	A/P	A/S
Bernard		P	A/P	A/S	A/S	P	P	A/S	A/S
June		P	A	P	A	P	P	P	A
Total main class enrollment		26	26	26	26	26	26	26	26
Total Present		20	18	19	21	18	19	19	19
Total Missing		6	8	7	5	8	7	7	7
New Members									
Paula		P	P	A/S	A/S	P	P	P	P
Total New Students		1	1	1	1	1	1	1	1
New Members Present		1	1	0	0	1	1	1	1
Total Missing		0	1	1	1	0	0	0	0
Total Students		27	27	27	27	27	27	27	27
Total Students Present		20	19	19	21	19	20	20	20
Total Students Missing		7	8	13	6	8	7	7	7
Guests Present		0	0	0	0	0	0	0	0
Total Guest Present		0	0	0	0	0	0	0	0
Grand Total Present		20	19	19	21	19	20	20	20

Unless new members are attending your class, you are not growing.

Appendix III

Age Group Roll Call

There are several things to understand about the roll call. Going across it, you will see the student's name and phone number. The date is for Sunday school attendance, and "MW" stands for midweek Bible study. The letter P shows who is present; A/P reflects those who are late. A/P can also represent other things like "A/ sick," "A/vacation," since the letter A just means absent. Studying this roll call can give you a lot of information about your students, like who's present, who's late, and who's sick. This roll call will help you see the improvement you are looking for, or it will show you where your group needs to improve. Try it; you just might like it!

My 20- - GIVING COMMITMENT

NAME   MR.   MISS   MR. & MRS. _____ Date_____

I (we) want to see New Life become a **Cutting Edge Church** through giving. With the help of God, my (our) giving commitment for this year of will be as follows:

My (our) Tithes will be $ _____   wkly,   bi-wkly,   mthly   (circle one please)

My (our) Offering will be $ _____   wkly,   bi-wkly,   mthly   (circle one please)

My (our) LDH will be $ _____   wkly,   bi-wkly,   mthly   (circle one please)

My (our) Midweek will be $ _____   wkly,   bi-wkly,   mthly   (circle one please)

Circle your age group:

Age groups: 11-12   13-18   19-24   25-31   32-37   38-46   47-52   53-58   59-65   66+

Appendix IV

Age Group Yearly Income Commitment Card

Appendix Y

Mission:
*Equipping Church Leaders
for Effective Ministry
Ephesians 4:12*

Dr. Addis Moore ~ *President*

*Theme 20[...]
Solidarity With the Savior in Service and Sacri[...]
1 Corinthians 3:9[...]
Philippians 2:[...]*

Website: www.wolverinestatecongress.[...]
Email: mipresmoore@mtzionkalamazoo.[...]

March 16, 2012

Rev. Rufus Bradley, Sr.
Pastor
New Life Ministries
1401 Janes Avenue
Saginaw, MI 48601

Dear Pastor Bradley:

Re: Developing Shepherd Leaders, Growth Through Multiplication

The Shepherd program presented at Mt. Zion Baptist Church to our Leadership Team was thoroughly developed, tried and tested, and proven to achieve results. I was attracted to the program based on the results I personally witnessed at New Life Ministries.

This program gave us an innovative, biblical way to engage leaders to build additional leaders to grow the church. The program connects people to people and makes the process of discipleship seamless and engaging. This program will be an excellent tool to share with the pastors and leaders at the Wolverine State Congress of Christian Education.

I believe that this program is perfect for any pastor who is serious about getting biblical results. This program, if used as presented, will not only transform the church, but it will cause the church to transform the community in which it resides.

I thank God for Pastor Rufus Bradley, Sr., his spiritual insight, and continual willingness to help churches build great ministries.

Partnering Together for Kingdom Building,

Dr. Addis Moore
President

cac

CITY OF
SAGINAW

1315 S. Washington Avenue
Saginaw, MI 48601

March 11, 2012

Pastor Rufus Bradley, Sr.
Mission in the City
1401 Janes Avenue
Saginaw, MI 48601

Dear Pastor Bradley:

As I have said many times throughout my six years on City Council, Saginaw is in the midst of a rebirth, and that we are on our way to making Saginaw, once again, a great city.

Your work is one of the reasons I can say that.

If there's one thing we've learned over the last 50 years, it's that we cannot count on government – at any level – to solve all our problems ... particularly as governmental resources grow more and more scarce. We will only grow and thrive through the efforts of the business and faith-based communities and the citizens who, working together with government, make great things happen.

Mission in the City is an excellent example. You had a clear vision and, more importantly, the dedication and willingness to work that brings a vision to life. And what a vision it is. It has brought a new vibrancy to a neighborhood that needed it badly. It has instilled a sense of pride and ownership in people who have sought it for many years. And it has reminded everyone – from the neighbors who surround it to others throughout the City – that great things happen when we work together.

I congratulate you and all who have worked with you to make Mission in the City a reality. I have found it both a pleasure and an inspiration to work with you, and I thank you for your efforts to make Saginaw a better place.

Sincerely,

Greg Branch
Mayor

Appendix VII

MICHIGAN HOUSE OF REPRESENTATIVES

STACY ERWIN OAKES

STATE REPRESENTATIVE

99TH DISTRICT
STATE CAPITOL
P.O. BOX 30014
LANSING, MI 48909-7514
PHONE: (517) 373-0152
FAX: (517) 373-8738
E-MAIL: stacyerwinoakes@house.mi.gov

July 26, 2011

Pastor Rufus Bradley, Sr.,
New Life Ministries
1401 Janes Ave.
Saginaw, MI 48601

Dear Pastor Bradley,

It is with great pleasure that I commend you, New Life Ministries and the Mission in the City Movement for the positive action which you have generated in the Saginaw Community. Hearing the voice of our residents, you were moved to action and began the arduous task of bringing the New Life Baptist Church Sports and Fitness Park into being. You have created a model for other motivated civic and religious groups to follow not only in the city but also in the state.

In addition the much needed recreation space which this park provides, it also adds to the beautification of the city itself. It also provides a safe, clean and supervised place for youth to play and for families and neighbors to congregate and engage in outdoor activity.

I truly admire the sense of civic-mindedness which you as pastor have imparted in your congregation. If there is ever any way that I can be of assistance, please do not hesitate to contact my office.

Yours in Service,

Stacy Erwin Oakes

Stacy Erwin Oakes
State Representative
District 95

Appendix VIII

World Outreach Campus

OFFICE
2405 Bay St.
Saginaw, MI 48602

PHONE
989-752-2955

FAX
989-752-9464

EMAIL
hurleycoleman@yahoo.com

WEB
www.thewoc.org

June 27, 2012
Rev. Rufus Bradley
New Life Baptist Church

Dear Pastor Bradley,

I have been back in the city of Saginaw since the summer of 2001 in the capacity of Pastor. It has been an interesting experience. My prior career was in the public arena of parks and recreation. I held several positions in cities and counties and understand the value of quality of life investments in communities.

One of the most significant things that I have seen is the Mission in the City project that has been developed by your church. It follows the path that I have seen throughout my career.

I have seen parks and recreation facilities improve the morale of the residents, increase economic investment from the private sector as well as public dollars. In each of these situations, it was the result of the vision and effort of one person.

Vision is a powerful thing. One person sees a deteriorating neighborhood, vacant houses, and scrabbled lawns. You saw a vibrant recreation facility and children active in positive social interaction.

One facility of this sort can change the entire atmosphere in a neighborhood. It happened in Inkster, where we built a golf course, and in Detroit where we built a wave pool.

There is no limit to the good that your efforts will do. I commend you.

Sincerely yours,

Hurley J. Coleman, Jr.

Pastor

Appendix IX

Mt. Zion Baptist Churc

Our Vision: A Church Living in Obedience to God's
Our Mission: Growing God's Kingdom According To His

September 2, 2011

Rev. Rufus Bradley, Sr., Pastor
New Life Ministries
1401 Janes Avenue
Saginaw, MI 48601

Dear Pastor Bradley:

Thank you for founding the "Mission in the City Movement" in Saginaw. My heart will always be invested in the Saginaw community, being a former resident. This initiative is a wonderful example for Saginaw to be a happier and more productive community.

After attending the Grand Opening of The Sports and Fitness Park on June 11, I was excited how this Park will bring awareness on health, exercise, and lifestyle changes. It is a place for young people to get off the streets and have activities within a safe and structured environment. It also invites neighborhoods and families to fellowship with one another with activities available (picnicking, jogging, walking, basketball, soccer, and others). Additionally, as President of the Wolverine State Congress of Christian Education which includes more than 700 churches on record, I am certain that this endeavor will serve as an inspiration and encouragement of what other churches can do in their communities. I will continually highlight the example of the rebirth of a community through Pastor Bradley and New Life Ministries.

It has been reported by the Center of Disease Control, the Center of Minority Health, the Department of Health and Human Services, National Institute of Health Services, and many others that a great majority of African American communities with moderate and low-income individuals   health is adversely affected by the lack of exercise (medications, high blood pressure, high cholesterol, obesity, kidney failure, stroke, stress, etc). The Park will greatly improve the health and possibly prevent adverse health conditions and diseases for individuals living in the Saginaw community.

It reads in 3 John 2, *Beloved, I pray that you may prosper in all things and be in health, just as your soul prospers.* Everyone who uses the Park will be blessed, and I foresee this Park being a stepping stone for other communities.

Partnering Together in Christ,

Dr. Addis Moore, Pastor

Appendix X

New Life Church
Mission in the City
Summer Youth Program
1401 Janes St.
Saginaw, MI 48601

To Whom it May Concern,   September 14, 2011

On behalf of Health Delivery, Inc and the School-Based Health Centers of Saginaw High School and Arthur Hill High School, I would like to say "thank you" for allowing us to partner with you for your Summer Youth Program. Through your program we were able to teach adolescents the importance of delaying sexual activity, as well as provide them with the skills needed to refuse peer pressure. The students also learned the seriousness of HIV and other STIs and how they could protect themselves from getting these diseases. All of the students reported that they had never engaged in sexual activity, and I believe that this is the ideal time to have this discussion with students. It is important to equip them with the knowledge and skills needed to face peer pressure, and I appreciate your willingness to let me come in and speak on such a sensitive topic. Please consider our program next year when you are planning your summer agenda. I would love to keep this dialogue open. Thank you for all you do for the community of Saginaw, especially our students!

Sincerely,

Amanda M. Forsmark, MHE, BA
Health Educator
Health Delivery, Inc
School-Based Health Centers
989-928-3311
aforsmark@healthdelivery.org

Appendix XI

Does Mentoring Work?

The stats prove what can happen if people take time out to mentor the youth in their communities. When you really look at the big picture, you can see it is exactly what we need to save the youth in our communities.

Mentoring Does Work!

In a Pew Public/Private Ventures Study of 959 boys and girls with 60 percent being members of a minority group, 60 percent boys, and 80 percent from low-income households, 487 were matched with mentors, and the remaining 472 were the control group with no mentors. After eighteen months with mentors, an evaluation of these children revealed:

- 46 percent were less likely to use illegal drugs
- 27 percent were less likely to use alcohol
- 37 percent were less likely to skip class
- 53 percent were less likely to skip school
- 33 percent were less likely to hit someone

More Statistics on Mentoring

A study by Proctor and Gamble of mentoring in Cincinnati schools showed young people with mentors were more likely to:

- Stay in school
- Attend classes
- Be less disruptive when attending class
- Get better grades
- Go to college

A Ford Foundation study of high school students from families receiving public assistance found those with mentors were more likely than those without mentors to:

- Graduate from high school
- Enroll in college
- Have fewer children
- Have fewer arrests
- Live without public assistance
- Become involved in community service
- Be hopeful about their future

California Mentor Foundation surveyed 124 mentor programs with 36,251 mentors and 57,659 mentees. The survey showed:

- 98 percent stayed in school
- 85 percent did not use drugs
- 98 percent were deterred from teen pregnancy
- 98 percent did not join a gang[16]

---

16 These stats and others can be found at this website:
www.beamentor.org/Taxdeductible2.htm.

Appendix XII

The Benefits of Basketball

Ten Benefits of Basketball:

- Burns calories
- Builds up muscles and tones the body
- Can be a great cardiovascular workout
- Builds endurance
- Increases flexibility, speed, and agility
- Improves coordination
- Develops good team player attitude
- Develops concentration and self-discipline
- Enhances confidence
- Helps you make new friends[17]

---

17 This information can be found at this website:
www.basketball.factoidz.com/ten-benefits-of-basketball.

Appendix XIII

The Benefits of Walking

- Lowers low-density lipoprotein (LDL) cholesterol (the "bad" cholesterol)
- Raises high-density lipoprotein (HDL) cholesterol (the "good" cholesterol)
- Lowers your blood pressure
- Reduces your risk of or manage type-2 diabetes
- Manages your weight
- Improves your mood
- Helps to stay strong and fit

All it takes to reap these benefits is a routine of brisk walking. It doesn't get much simpler. And you can forget the "no pain, no gain" talk. Research shows a regular, brisk walk can reduce the risk of heart attack by the same amount as more vigorous exercise, such as jogging.[18]

---

18 This information can be found at this website, www.mayoclinic.com.

Appendix XIV

Sports and Fitness Park Rules

- No fighting
- No wrestling/horseplay
- No weapons
- No foul language
- No smoking
- No drinking
- No drugs
- No damage to the park
- No disrespecting neighbors
- No disrespecting leaders/mentors
- No sagging pants
- No revealing clothing
- No gambling
- No loitering

- No polluting
- No soliciting
- No pets
- No climbing the fence
- No dunking/hanging on basketball rims
- No bikes, scooters, skates, skateboards, etc.
- No duffel bags
- Or any other inappropriate behaviors not listed
- *Clothes/shoes must be worn at all times!*
- Those whose behavior cannot be controlled will be asked to leave or will be handled by law enforcement.

Appendix XV

Department of Development • 1315 South Washington Avenue • Saginaw, Michigan 48601

March 28, 2012

New Life Baptist Church
Pastor Rufus Bradley, Sr.
1401 Janes Street
Saginaw, MI 48601

RE: MISSION IN THE CITY COMMUNITY DEVELOPMENT ORGANIZATION

Dear Pastor Bradley:

As the Director of Development for the City of Saginaw, I am writing this letter in support of the Mission in the City Community Development Organization. Mission in the City is designed to work towards improving and restoring the community one person, one block at a time, ultimately creating a program that addresses the needs of the community.

On behalf of the City of Saginaw, we appreciate the difference you have made through various events such as: The Health Walk, Sports & Fitness Park, Youth Camp, Community Basketball and the 1st Annual Community Picnic. Mission in the City has also played a vital role in assisting the City of Saginaw on one of its top priorities, removing blight and neighborhood revitalization.

Mission in the City has truly blessed many lives with its tireless work ethic, dedication and persistence to make Saginaw a better place to live, work and raise a family.

Pastor Bradley and the entire membership of New Life Baptist Church, we deeply appreciate the positive impact you have made in our community through the Mission in the City Development Organization and extend immense congratulations on a job well done!

Sincerely,

Odail Thorns
Director of Development

About the Author

Pastor Rufus Bradley Sr. is a graduate of United Theological Seminary in (Monroe, Louisiana), where he earned a Bachelor's Degree in Religious Education. He has also completed an Advanced Leadership Training Program to enhance his skills in the areas of visionary leadership, mentoring, theoretical and practical knowledge, provided by the Beeson Institute, a program of Asbury Theological Seminary. Pastor Bradley also received an honorary doctorate of Divinity from Union Baptist Seminary, Inc., in Birmingham, Alabama in July of 2012 for his insight and commitment to the rehabilitation and sustainability of the community.

He is also the founder of "Mission in The City a community development organization" where he has received numerous awards and statewide recognition for community enhancement including a community sports and fitness park for the community as part of God's new direction for his ministry life.